AF584532

What on Earth! is an imprint of What on Earth Publishing.
The Black Barn, Wickhurst Farm, Tonbridge, Kent, TN11 8PS, United Kingdom
30 Ridge Road Unit B, Greenbelt, Maryland, 20770, United States

First published in hardback in the United Kingdom in 2023
This paperback edition published in the United Kingdom in 2026

Text copyright © 2023 What on Earth Publishing Ltd. and Britannica, Inc.
Illustrations copyright © 2023 Andy Smith
Trademark notices on page 204. Picture credits on page 207.

All rights reserved. No part of this publication may be reproduced or transmitted in any form or by any means, electronic or mechanical, including photocopying, recording, or any information storage or retrieval system, without permission in writing from the publishers. Requests for permission to make copies of any part of this work should be directed to info@whatonearthbooks.com.

Written by Julie Beer
Illustrated by Andy Smith
Designed by Lawrence Morton
Text developed by WonderLab Group, LLC
Project edited by Judy Barratt
Picture research by Annette Kiesow
Indexed by Connie Binder
Fact-checked by Michele Rita Metych

Andy Smith has asserted his right to be identified as illustrator under the Copyright, Designs and Patents Act 1988.

What on Earth!
Natalie Bellos, Publisher; Alison Eldridge, Editor; Charka Stout, Assistant Editor;
Andrew Forshaw, Art Director; Alenka Oblak, Production Manager

A CIP catalogue record for this book is available from the British Library

ISBN: 9781804661970

Printed in China
DC/Shenzhen, China/01/2026

EU Authorised Representative: Easy Access System Europe – Mustamäe tee 50, 10621 Tallin, Estonia,
gpsr.requests@easproject.com

10 9 8 7 6 5 4 3 2 1

whatonearthbooks.com

ANIMAL FACTopia!

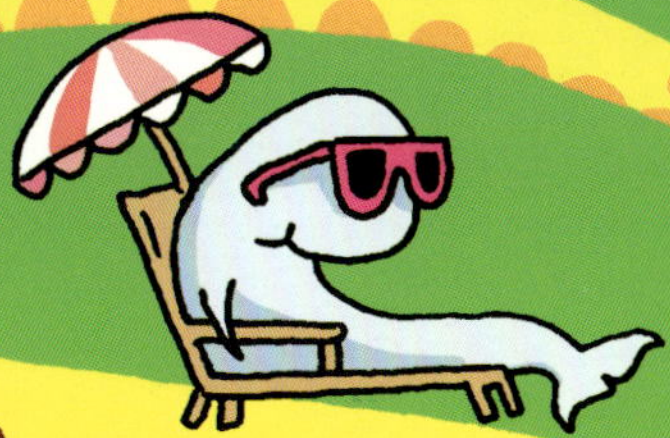

Follow the TRAIL of 400 BEASTLY FACTS

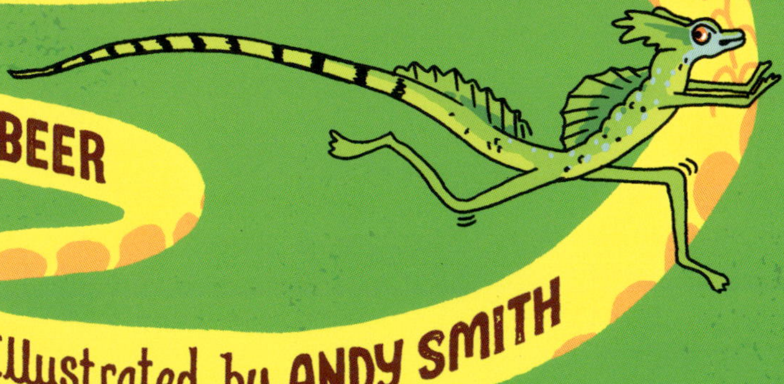

BY JULIE BEER

What on Earth!

CONTENTS

ROAR, FLY and SLITHER back to FACTopia!

Get ready, because things are about to get wild.

Prepare for a fact-filled animal adventure that explores hundreds of Earth's feathery, scaly, creepy, cuddly and dangerous creatures. For example...

Did you know ants don't have ears? They 'listen' by feeling vibrations with their legs.

Get a leg up on more. Like the strawberry poison frog, which is red all over except for its bright blue legs – the source of its nickname, the 'blue jeans' frog.

They're not the only things that are blue. An Arctic reindeer's eyes change from gold in the summer to deep blue during the chilly winter.

Brr! Keep cosy with survival strategies from amazing animals like the Arctic fox, which wraps its fluffy tail around its body like a blanket to stay warm.

You might have spotted that there is something special about being here in FACTopia. Every fact is *linked to the next*, and in the most surprising and even hilarious ways.

On this FACTopia adventure you will discover creatures from the **deepest seas** to the **hottest deserts** to **grand grasslands** – and even beasts that roamed Earth in **prehistoric times**. Discover what each turn of the page will bring!

But there isn't just one trail through this book. Your path branches every now and then, and you can **hop backwards** or **gallop forwards** → to a totally different (*but still connected*) part of FACTopia.

Let your curiosity take you wherever it leads. Of course, a good place to start could be right here, at the beginning......

For example, take this detour

to find out about perfect paws

Go to page 184

A newborn female African elephant weighs about as much as...

Speaking of elephants
...28 newborn human babies.

African elephants gain the nickname '**tuskers**' when their tusks grow so long they touch the ground

e equivalent of 33 glasses of water in its trunk at one time.
Elephants can
SNORT
Listen closely

ALLIGATORS SOMETIMES MAKE A COUGH-LIKE SOUND CALLED A CHUMPF.

WALRUSES CAN MAKE A WHISTLING SOUND THAT RESEMBLES A HUMAN'S WHISTLE.
Whistle a tune!

A lanternfish's **body** has organs that emit light, allowing the fish to **glow** in the dark.

When threatened, the walnut sphinx caterpillar compresses itself like an accordion, letting out a shrill whistling sound from holes along the sides of its **body**.

Fireflies can **glow** green, yellow and **orange**.

Green sea **turtles** get their name from the green-coloured **fat** found under their shells.

The fossilised **shell** of one of the biggest **turtles** ever discovered is nearly 2.4 metres long and has fighting horns near its neck.

In the winter, hibernating dwarf lemurs from Madagascar survive on the **fat** stored in their **tails**.

The rattle on the end of a rattlesnake's **tail** is made of keratin, the same material that makes up hooves, **horns** and human hair.

A type of extinct deerlike animal that lived in Florida about five million years ago had a **horn** on its **nose** shaped like a slingshot.

When opossums are under attack, they stick out their **tongues** and produce a foul **smell**, appearing to be dead.

Gentoo penguins have **orange tongues** covered in spiky bristles that help them grip and swallow fish whole.

Giving off an odour that **smells** like watermelon helps the hooded nudibranch, a species of **marine slug**, fend off predators.

Female argonaut octopuses, also called paper nautiluses, carry their **eggs** inside a special **shell** they build themselves out of a mineral secreted by their own arms.

Sea lemons are a type of **marine slug** that lay up to two million **eggs** in a structure that looks like a ribbon.

The nostrils on the **noses** of some animals like moose, hippos and manatees close automatically when submerged **underwater**.

Tweet, tweet!

American dippers walk **underwater**! These birds are often spotted walking along the bottom of a river or stream looking for insects.

Go to page 108

One hundred million years ago, **birds had teeth**

Chomp down

A group of goldfinches is called a **charm**

A male white bellbird has a long piece of skin, called a wattle, that hangs from its beak. But that doesn't stop it from being the **loudest bird** on the planet. Its call is as loud as the sound coming out of a speaker at a rock concert

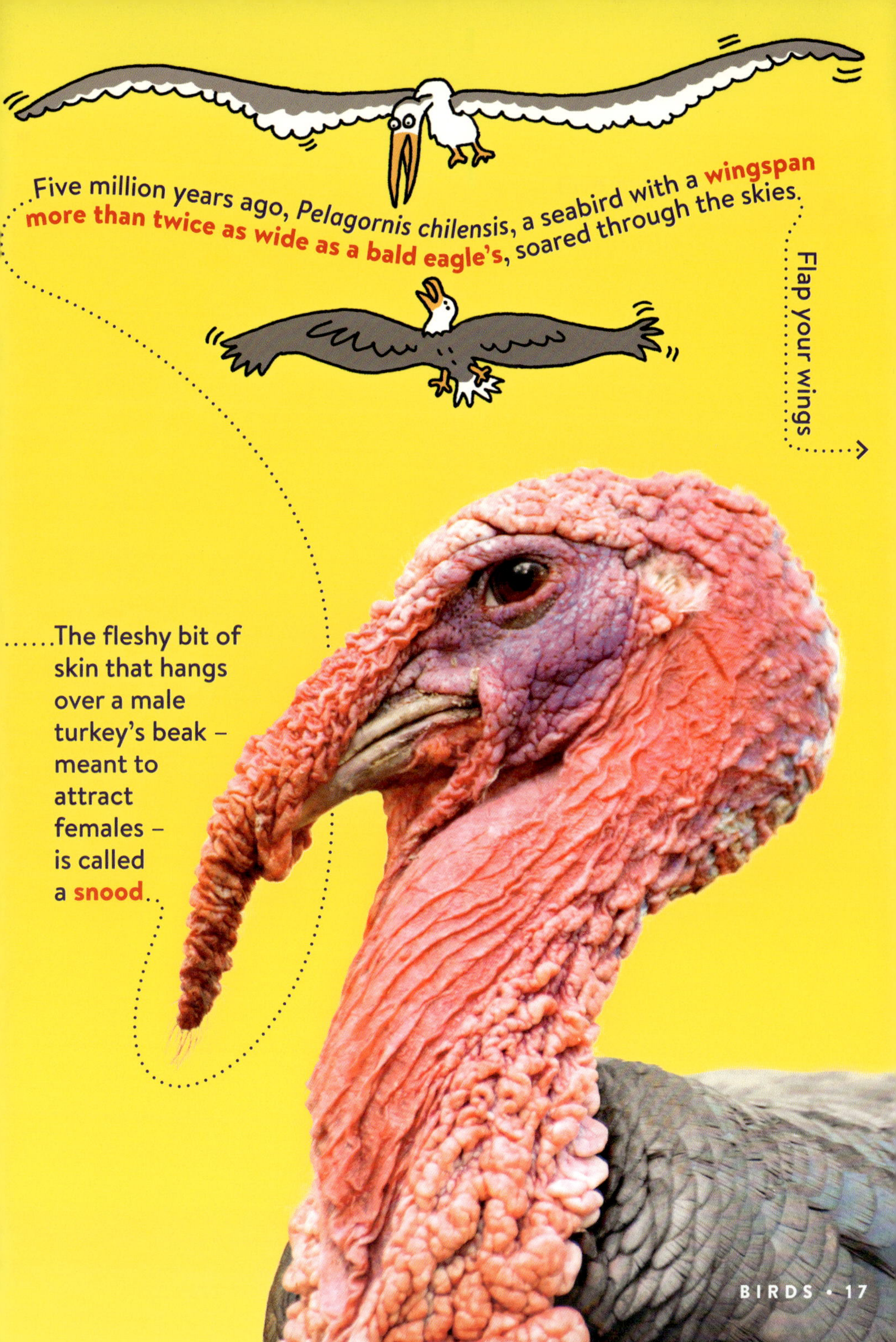
Five million years ago, *Pelagornis chilensis*, a seabird with a **wingspan more than twice as wide as a bald eagle's**, soared through the skies.
Flap your wings
The fleshy bit of skin that hangs over a male turkey's beak – meant to attract females – is called a **snood**.

The temperature needs to be at least 13 degrees Celsius for a monarch butterfly's wings to warm up – **otherwise it can't fly**.

Some animals don't need wings to soar

The colugo is called a '**flying lemur**', even though it can't actually fly and it isn't a lemur. Instead of jumping, colugos glide from tree to tree using the skin between their limbs like a wingsuit, looking for their next meal of leaves and fruit ...

The largest species of flying squirrels, which glide between trees, is as **big as a house cat** ...

Flying fish use their **winglike fins and fork-shaped tails** to glide throu

Go to page 190

Ribbit, ribbit

Sugar gliders **leap through forests at night.** They bob their heads before they 'take off' to help them determine distance and altitude.

More night owls

Wallace's flying frogs have **extra skin between their toes** to help them glide between tree branches, and oversized toe pads to help them stick when they land.

the air. Some can 'fly' the length of about 15 double-decker buses.

Fabulous feet
Go to page 122

Scorpions
glow blue-green
under ultraviolet light...
If you shine a torch on
a spider at night, its
eyes glow green.
Eye spy

An Arctic reindeer's eyes change from
gold
in the summer to
DEEP BLUE
in the winter.

Red-eyed tree frogs sleep camouflaged on green leaves, but if disturbed they flash their bulging red eyes, **startling predators**.

Snow leopards can **leap** the length of four Sumatran **rhinos** in one stride.

Great white sharks can **leap** completely out of the water while attacking prey.

Humans and **giraffes** have the same number of **bones** in their necks – seven!

Orcas are considered the top predator of the ocean – sometimes scaring away **great white sharks** from their hunting grounds.

Fossilised dinosaur **bones** can be **smelly**.

White rhinos and black rhinos are the same colour – grey.

To impress females, male blue-footed boobies show off the bright colour of their feet by doing a high-stepped dance.

The back of a giraffe has a small hump on it, similar to a camel's.

Some swan species swim with one of their feet tucked on their backs.

The male ring-tailed lemur, native to the African island of Madagascar, produces a smelly substance from its wrists, rubs it on its tail, and then waves its tail in the air to attract mates.

Island life

There are about **five sheep for every person** on the islands of New Zealand
The Hawaiian name for the Hawaiian monk seal is **`Ilio-holo-I-ka-uaua**, which means 'dog that runs in rough water'.

Go to page 106

Head to the farm

Marine iguanas of the Galápagos Islands **sneeze out extra salt** they ingest from their ocean environment, forming a white 'wig' on their head.

Looking for lizards

A Komodo dragon can weigh as much as a fridge.
The basilisk lizard can run on water for short distances to catch insects

nake a quick escape from a predator.

Make a getaway

One African penguin at a German zoo escaped and accidentally wandered into the lion enclosure. Fortunately, the **lions were all asleep**, and the zookeepers led the penguin to safety using a trail of fish.

Go to page 74

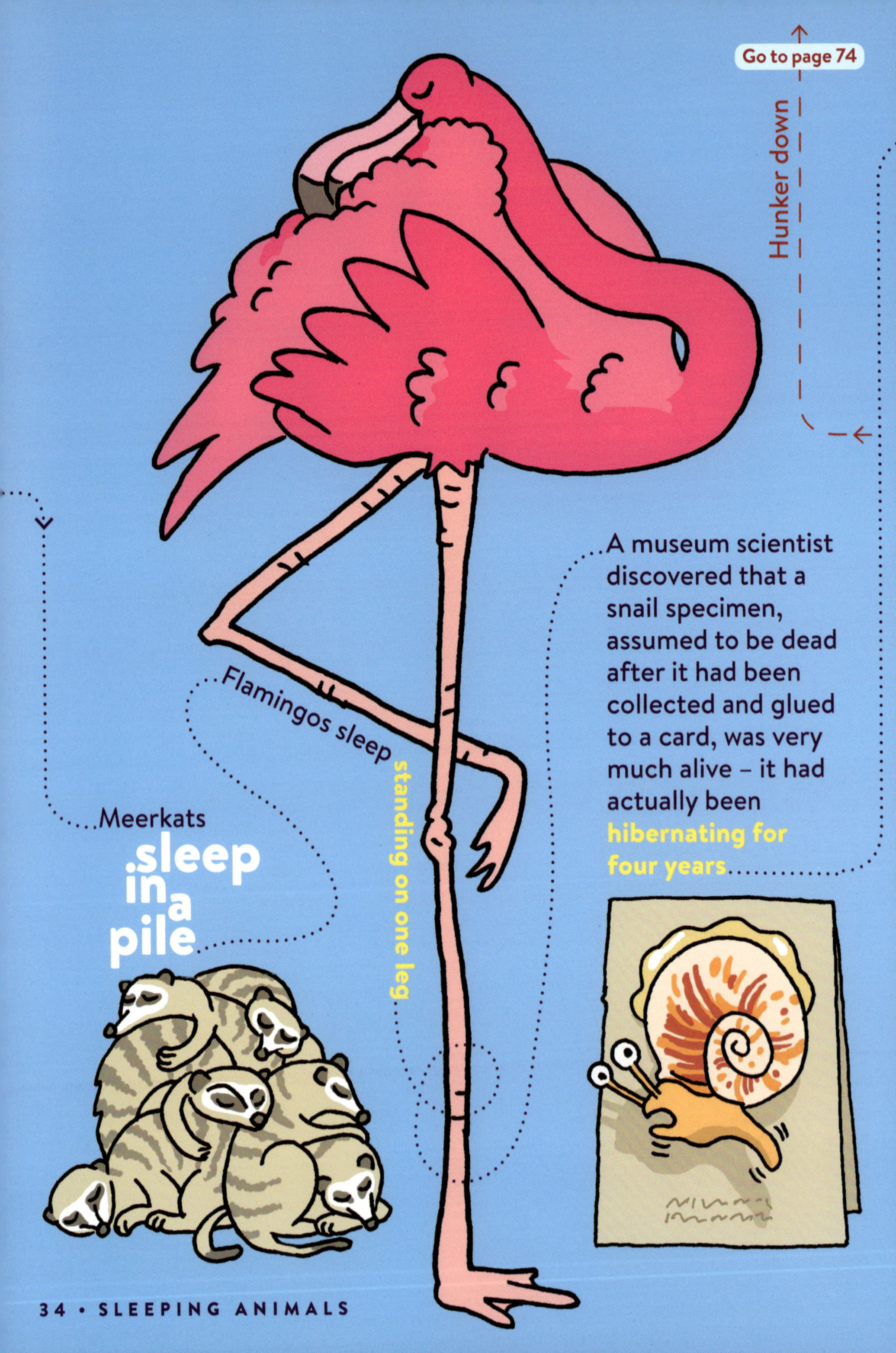

A museum scientist discovered that a snail specimen, assumed to be dead after it had been collected and glued to a card, was very much alive – it had actually been **hibernating for four years**

Bats can't take off from the ground.
So most bats sleep hanging upside down
to allow them to drop into flight straightaway.
Whale watching
Sperm whales sleep vertically
near the surface of the ocean

Beluga whales are
born grey – and then
turn white once they
become adults
A blue whale's mouth can fit 100 people inside

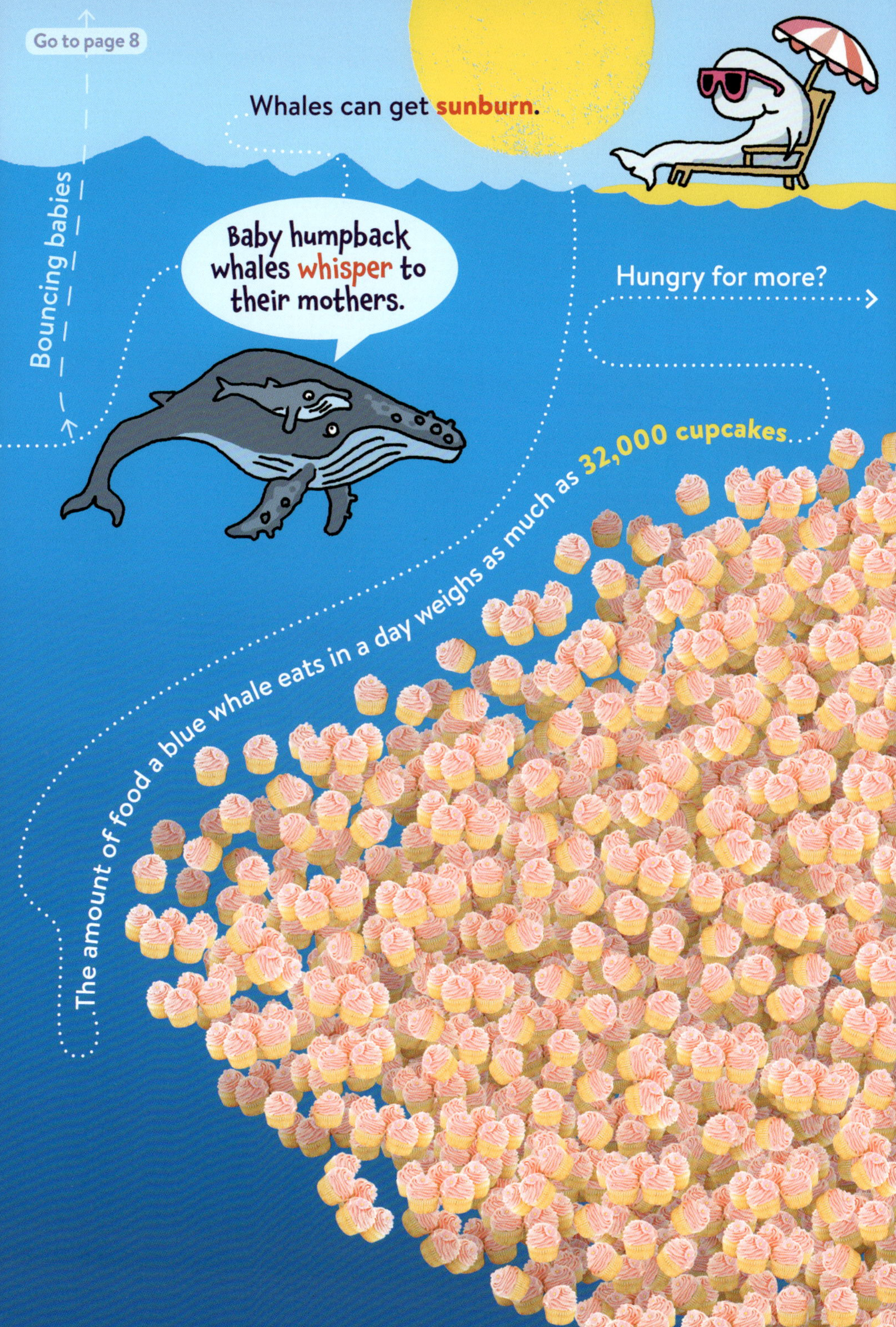

Go to page 8
Whales can get sunburn.
Bouncing babies
Baby humpback whales whisper to their mothers.
Hungry for more?
The amount of food a blue whale eats in a day weighs as much as 32,000 cupcakes.

Egg-eating snakes swallow eggs whole and then use special neck spines to break the eggshell and get at the contents inside. Then, they throw up the shell!
Platypuses don't have teeth, so they **scoop up rocks** into their cheeks to help them chew their food.

Go to page 78
Egg-cellent eggs
Super skin
Some types of baby caecilians – a legless amphibian – **eat their mothers' skin**

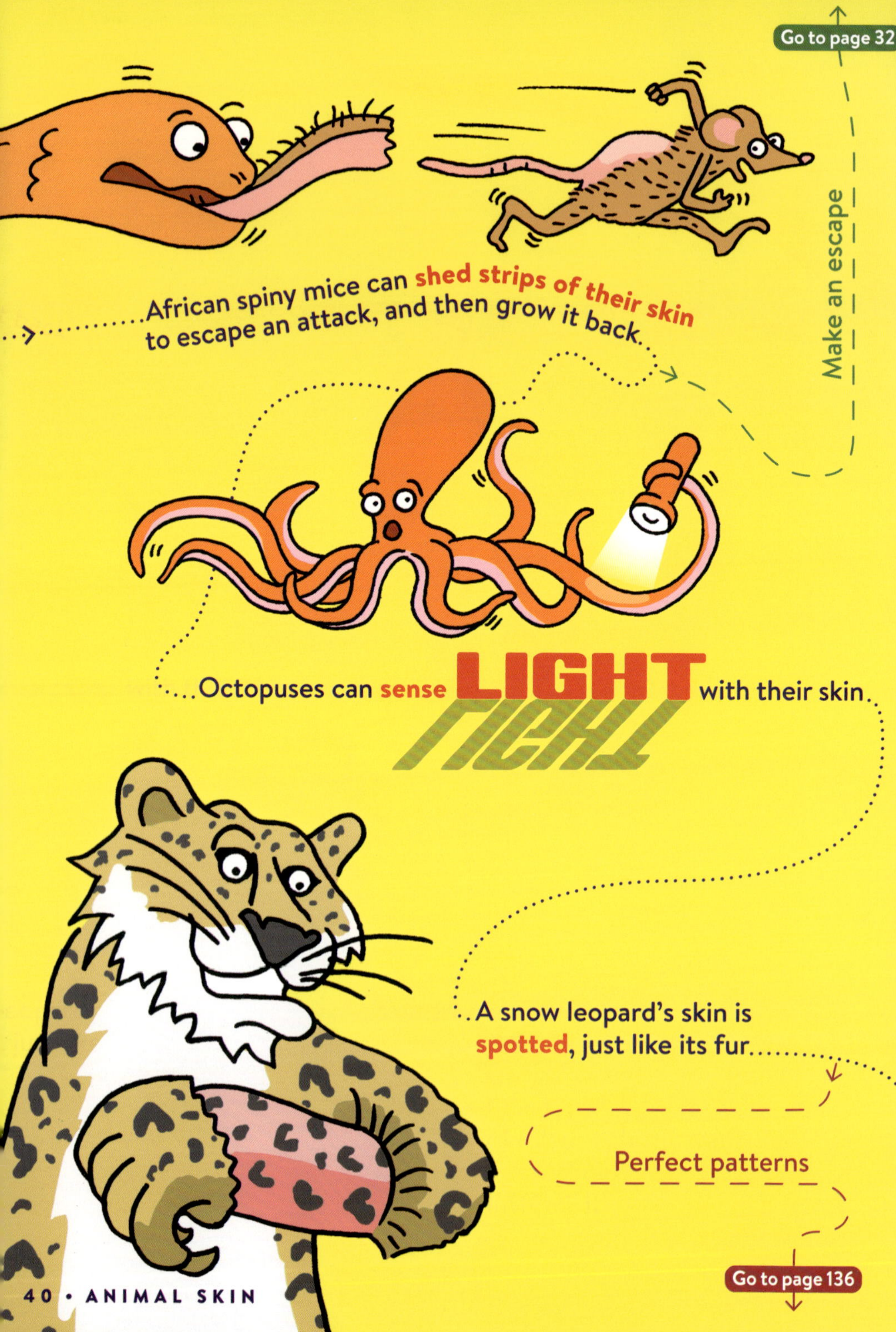

Go to page 32

African spiny mice can **shed strips of their skin** to escape an attack, and then grow it back.

Octopuses can **sense LIGHT** with their skin.

A snow leopard's skin is **spotted**, just like its fur.

Go to page 136

Chameleons **change the colour** of their skin
to help them cool down
or warm up
So colourful
One type
of salamander
has no lungs.
Instead, it
breathes through its skin

Sometimes, rare genetic mutations can cause penguins to be all **white or even yellow**.

Go to page 120

More bears

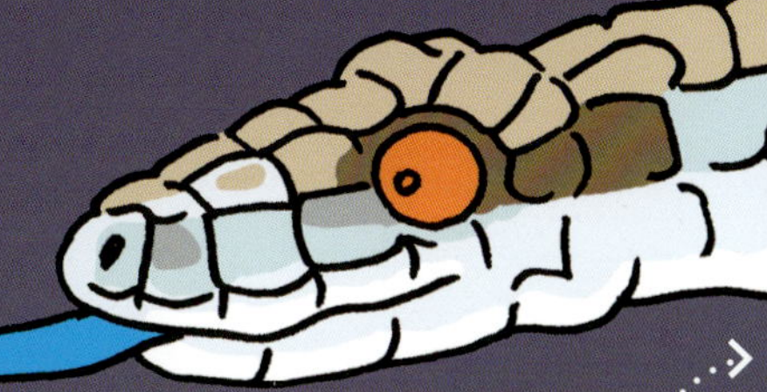

Blue-tongued skinks, a type of lizard, use their **brightly coloured tongues** to scare away predators.

More plants

Pink orchid praying mantises, named for the flowering plant they resemble, trick curious insects into investigating them. Then they eat them.

Peanut worms, which live in the ocean, have **purple blood**.

Pandas have unique **black eye patches** of different shapes and sizes that scientists think may help the pandas recognise each other.

One type of pitcher plant evolved to be a **toilet for treeshrews**. When the shrew visits, it eats the plant's nectar while sitting atop the toilet bowl-shaped plant and pooing into it, providing the plant with essential nutrients.

Bee orchids are **flowers that evolved to look like female bees** in order to attract male bees that pollinate the plant.

Incredible insects

A cricket's ears are **on its legs**

Some bumblebees can fly higher than Mount Everest is tall
Going up!

Run over to rodents
Go to page 160

Scientists analysed hair, poo and bone believed to be from **abominable snowmen**. It turns out the samples were from black and brown bears that live in the Himalayas, and a dog.
Red pandas have flexible ankles that let them **climb headfirst** down trees in mountain forests in Asia
Come on down
Some snakes in Asia survive their cold mountain habitats by living near **hot springs**.

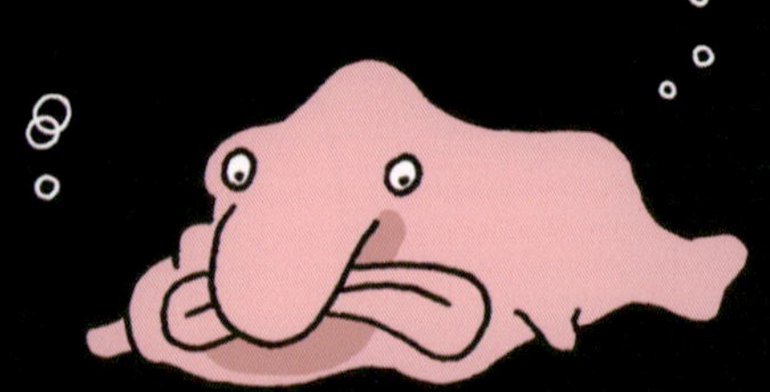

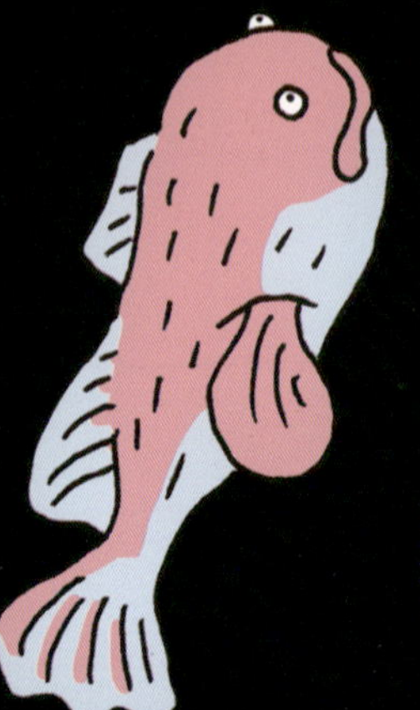

Blobfish don't have any muscles and look like pink oozy blobs at sea level. But in their high-pressure, deep-sea environment they look like normal swimming fish.

Giant tube worms make their homes next to **deep-sea hydrothermal vents** that spew superheated water and toxic chemicals.

Go to page 134

Fin-tastic fish

The female anglerfish, which lives in the deepest parts of the ocean, uses a **spine with a glowing tip above its head** as a lure to attract prey.

Poo, sand, decay and other bits that drift from the ocean's surface to the deep sea are called **marine snow**.

Let it snow

Because they are so hard to find, snow leopards are known as 'ghost cats',
Canadian lynx have oversized paws that act as snowshoes to keep them from sinking in the snow.
Cool cats
Go to page 82

Monkey around
Young snow monkeys play with snowballs.

A male proboscis monkey's

large nose

helps make its honking call louder, which warns enemies to stay away.

Go to page 114

After spending time apart, spider monkeys greet each other with a hug and **wrap their tails around one another.**

To catch fish

A cheetah's tail acts like a boat's rudder to help it change directions while sprinting.
Dash on
guars sometimes tap the surface of water with their tails, like a lure.

Dragonflies, the
FASTEST FLYING INSECTS,
catch 95 per cent of the prey they chase.
Sailfish speed through the water
as fast as a car drives on the motorway.
The mammal with
the fastest heartbeat is
the pygmy shrew at 1,200
beats per minute. That's about
15 times faster than
an average person's
resting heart
rate!

Australian tiger beetles are the world's **fastest running insects**. They can run farther than the length of a bicycle in one second.
Slow down
Greyhounds can accelerate **faster than horses**.

It can take up to a **whole month** for a sloth to digest its food
Moving at a snail's pace means covering a littl
Sunflower starfish have **15,000 feet** but can travel only about the length of three guitars in one minute

At its top speed, a **banana slug** takes one minute to cover the length of a banana ...

...more than the length of a skateboard in an hour.

Cool coral

Most **coral larvae** travel no more than 1.6 kilometres from their parents, take root on the ocean floor and never move again.

Fast-growing staghorn coral grow at about the **same speed as human hair**

Pygmy seahorses – which are smaller than a paper clip – spend their entire lives attached to coral. As babies, they grow bumps to match their habitat . . .

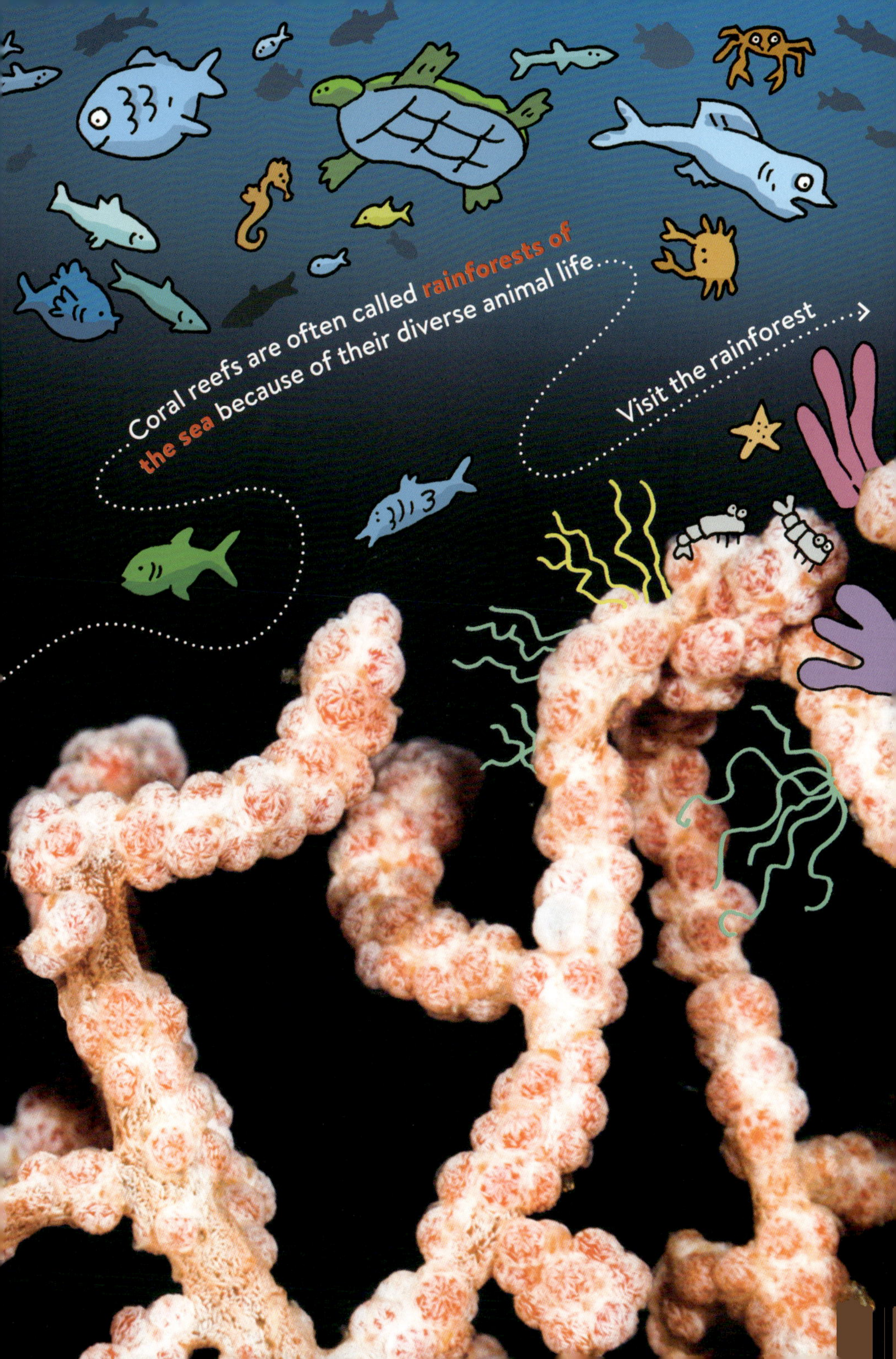
Coral reefs are often called **rainforests of the sea** because of their diverse animal life.
Visit the rainforest

Rainforest-dwelling **happy face spiders** can have a pattern that looks like a smiling face on their bodies.

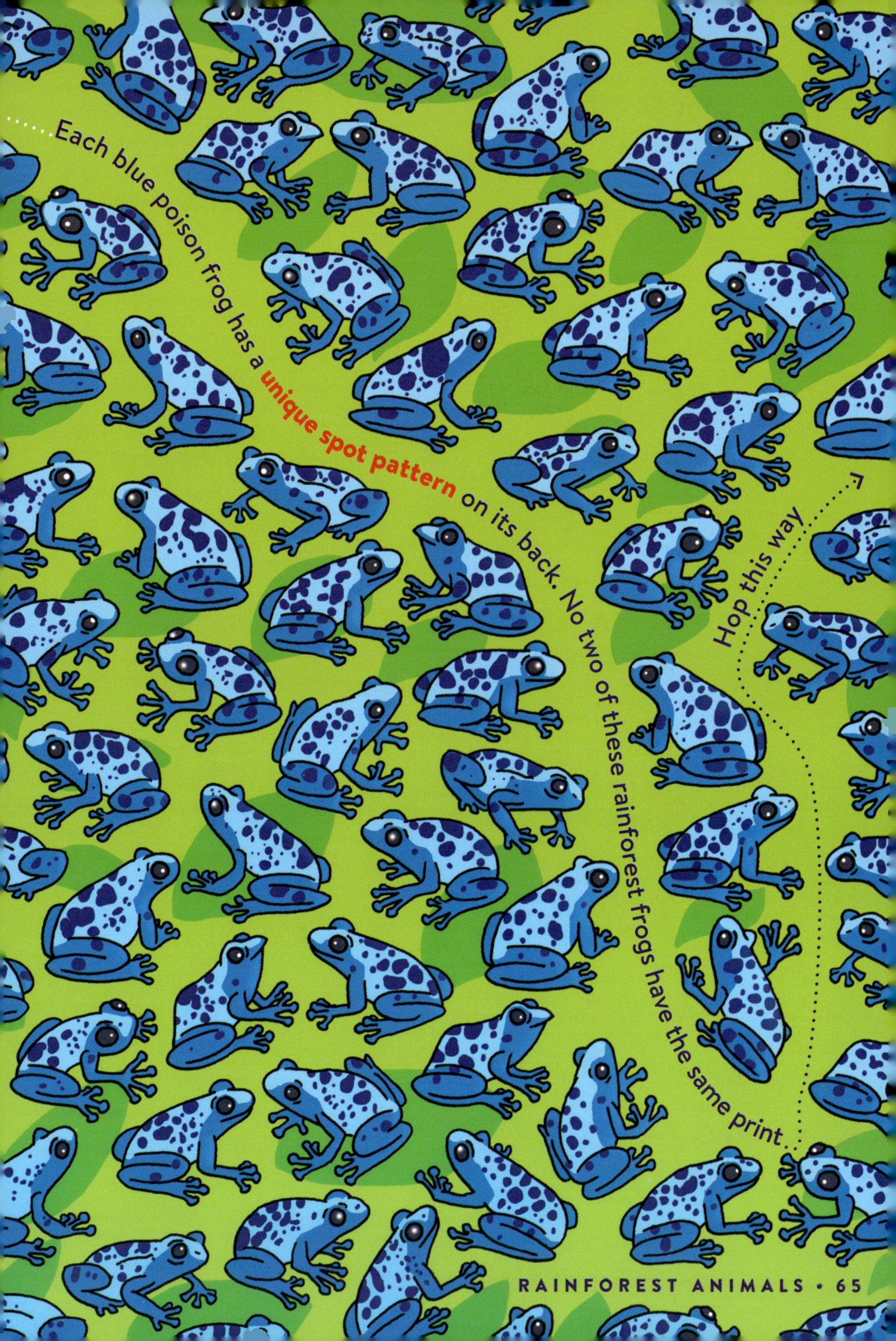
Each blue poison frog has a **unique spot pattern** on its back. No two of these rainforest frogs have the same print.
Hop this way

Facing each other and opening up their jaws as wide as they can is how male hippopotamuses size each other up before a fight.

While they are in the water, hippopotamuses are often followed by barbel fish, which nibble parasites off the hippos' skin, clean inside their mouths and even eat their poo!

The throat of a moray eel contains a second set of jaws.

A frog uses its eyes to help push food down its throat.

The northern Pinocchio tree frog gets its name from its long 'nose' – a fleshy spike that sticks out from its head.

A star-nosed mole finds prey using the 22 tentacles around its nose.

A fully grown male ostrich is tall enough for its head to reach the bottom of the net on an NBA basketball hoop.

The olm, a type of blind salamander that lives at the bottom of underwater caves, can survive 10 years without eating.

When it's time to **poo**, a three-toed **sloth** typically goes underneath the same tree each time. Scientists think it may help them communicate with other sloths... or fertilise trees they like.

Sloths eat the **green** algae that grow on their fur.

Green herons **drop** insects in water as bait to attract fish.

Egyptian vultures **drop** stones on ostrich eggs to **crack** them open.

Sea otters store a rock under their armpits to **crack** open **prey**, like clams.

Hanging from **cave** ceilings in Venezuela, giant **centipedes** prey on bats.

After the Peruvian giant yellow-leg **centipede** sheds its exoskeleton – or hard outer skin, which is longer than a pencil – it eats it.

Armour up!

An ironclad beetle's exoskeleton is so strong it can survive being

run over by a car

Beautiful beetles

Go to page 152

Glyptodon, an extinct relative of the armadillo with a **spiky club-shaped tail**, was so well covered in armour that even sabre-toothed cats had a hard time attacking it.

Giant ground sloths, which lived more than 13,000 years ago, ate AVOCADOS whole.
Edestus, a type of shark that had arcs of teeth on the roof and floor of its mouth, sliced through fish like a pair of scissors.

The dawn horse, **the first known horse,** was the size of a small dog.

A near-perfect woolly mammoth baby was found in Russia after being **frozen for 40,000 years**.

Chill out

Trot on over

Go to page 128

Microscopic tardigrades, also known as water bears, **can survive the extreme cold of space**

Antarctic midges – flightless insects – can survive being nearly **frozen solid** for nine months.

Antarctic emperor penguins **rock back and forth** on their heels to keep their feet from freezing.

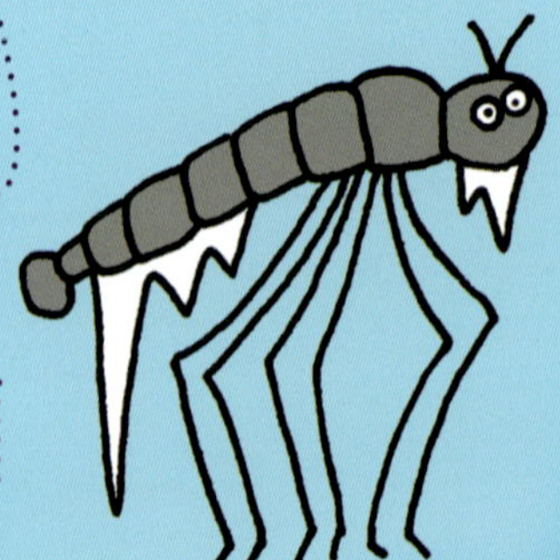

Teeny-tiny animals

Go to page 110

Arctic ground squirrels drop their body temperature down to below freezing while they are in a state of

HIBERNATION.

Time for a snooze

To keep warm in Arctic waters, beluga whales have a **layer of blubber** as thick as 10 slices of bread

Even when they're in a deep hibernation-like sleep, called torpor, **Australia's eastern pygmy possums** can sense danger, such as a wildfire ...

Down under

More **kangaroos than humans** live in Australia.

The shell of Australia's giant panda snail can grow to be as large as a tennis ball
An echidna lays a tiny egg the size of a grape, then keeps it in a pouch on its belly.
Crack open more

Prairie chickens, grassland animals, lay their eggs on nes

Horn sharks produce **spiral-shaped eggs**, which they screw into rocks and crevices with their mouths

tes called **booming grounds**, named after the low noise the male birds make.

Great grasslands

Skates, a type of fish related to rays, have **ravioli-shaped** egg cases

Zebras, which live in the grasslands
of eastern and southern Africa,
fart when they get startled.

Leopards sometimes carry their food high up in a tree to avoid it being stolen by other big cats or hyenas
On the prowl

Go to page 168

Félicette, a stray cat from France, was launched into space in 1963 for a 15-minute mission. Then her capsule slowly parachuted safely back to Earth.
Blast off!
Male cats are more likely to be left-pawed, and females are more likely to be right-pawed.

The Manatee Nebula, a giant cloud of gas and dust in space, got its name because it looks like a manatee floating on its back with its flippers crossed over its belly.

In the night sky, there are more dogs represented in the constellations than cats
Harbour seals are capable of using guide stars, called lodestars, to help them find their way when they're swimming far from shore
Dive in

A penguin's **BLACK-AND-WHITE 'TUXEDO'** helps it camouflage while swimming – its white belly blends with the sky when viewed from below, and its black back blends with dark water when viewed from above.

Look carefully

By staying very still and using their bumpy skin as camouflage, alligators ca

isguise themselves as floating logs when swimming in swamps and wetlands
Wild wetlands
Cuttlefish match not only the colour of their surroundings, but also the texture, like the rocky ocean floor

Go to page 86

Swim over

Swamp rabbits are excellent swimmers. They **jump in the water** to escape predators and dive to find food.

Like the hippo, the capybara – a relative of the guinea pig – has its eyes, ears and nose located high on its head, letting it **peek above water** while the rest of its body remains hidden.

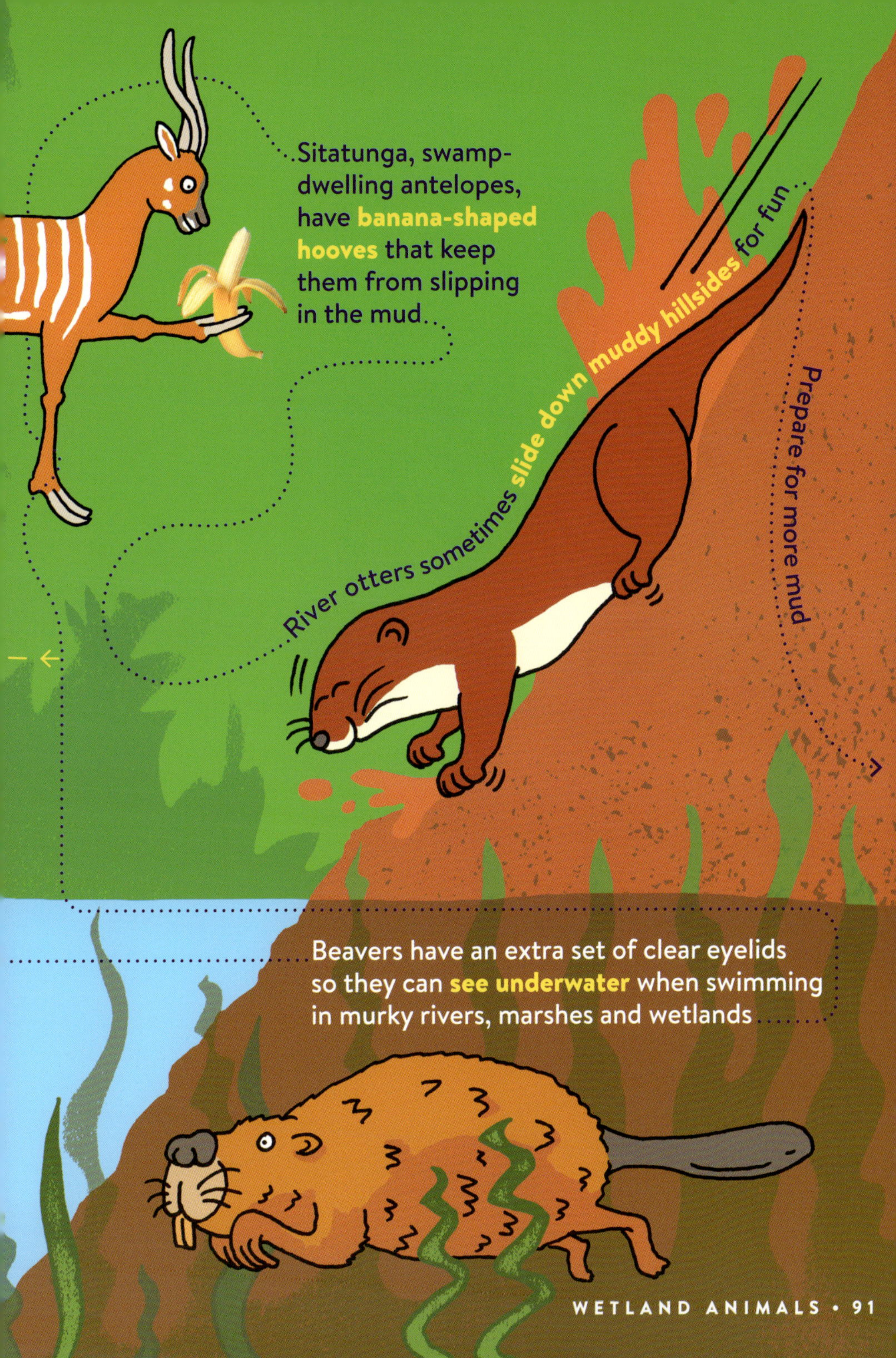
Sitatunga, swamp-dwelling antelopes, have **banana-shaped hooves** that keep them from slipping in the mud
River otters sometimes **slide down muddy hillsides** for fun
Prepare for more mud
Beavers have an extra set of clear eyelids so they can **see underwater** when swimming in murky rivers, marshes and wetlands

Mudpuppies, a type of salamander that lives on the muddy bottoms of rivers and ponds, can make a sound that resembles a

barking dog

Go to page 50

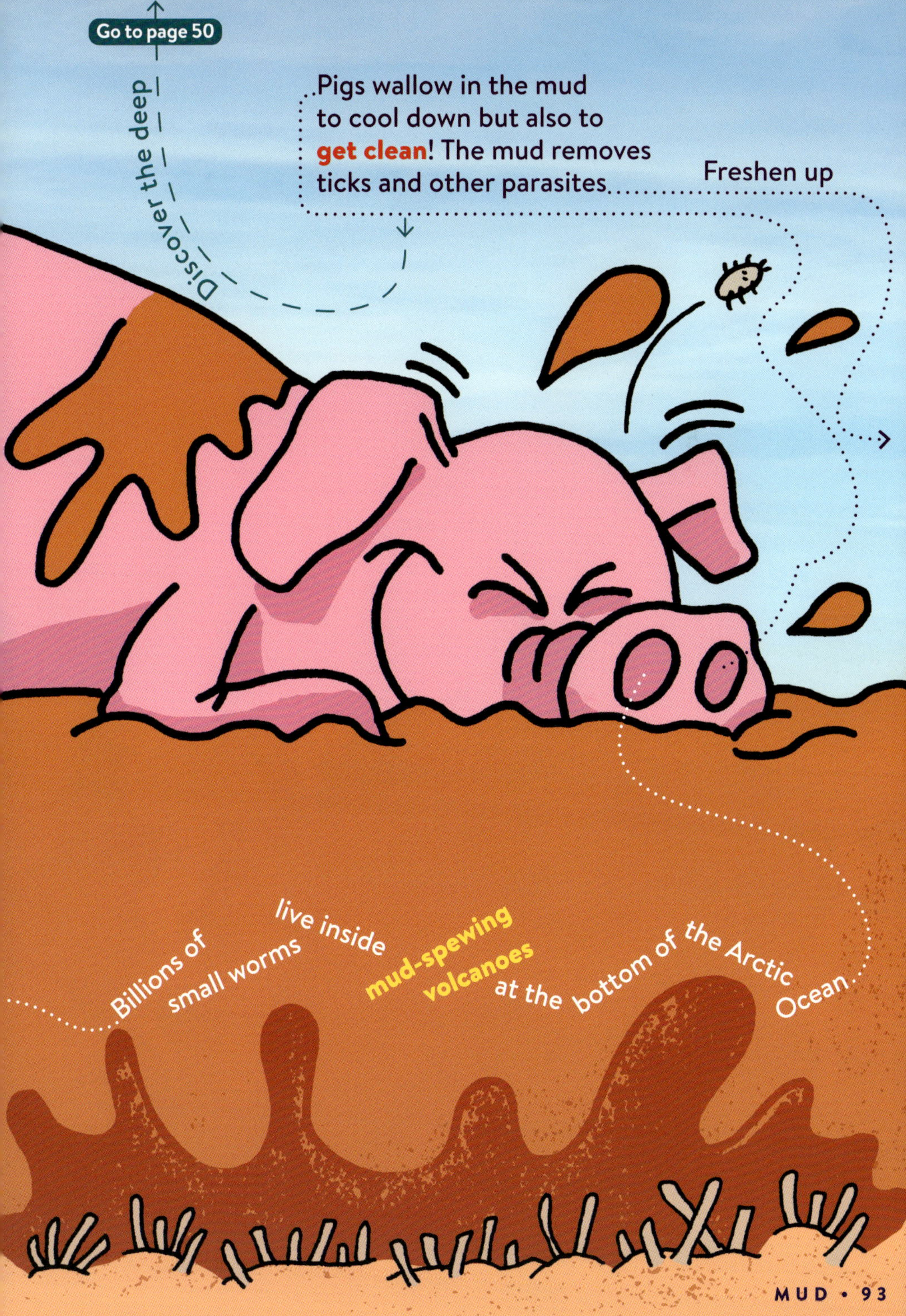
Discover the deep
Pigs wallow in the mud to cool down but also to **get clean**! The mud removes ticks and other parasites.
Freshen up
Billions of small worms live inside **mud-spewing volcanoes** at the bottom of the Arctic Ocean.

Go to page 54

Monkey mania

Apes and monkeys **pick lice out of each other's fur** and eat them

Japanese snow monkeys sometimes take baths in **hot springs**

Red and grey kangaroos prefer to eat and groom themselves with their **left paws**.

The babies of some bird species create a faecal sac, which is a case around their own poo. Their parents clean out these **bird 'diapers'** from the nest regularly by either dropping the sacs off somewhere else... or by eating them.

Get more goo
Go to page 180
It's getting hairy

The fur on a fennec fox's feet protects them from the desert's **hot sand**.

Female snow leopards **line their dens with their own fur** to keep their cubs warm.

Zebras that live in warmer climates have **more stripes**, which scientists think might keep them cooler.

Head home

Go to page 178

Go to page 138

The world's **loudest**

PURR

by a domestic cat measured as loud as a vacuum cleaner.

Polar bears have the largest paws of all bears – they're as wide as a **Frisbee**.

A Texas longhorn steer, a type of cow, set a world record for having horns that span **wider than the Statue of Liberty's head**

More head turners

Hearing things?

Go to page 12

Go to page 156

Kosmoceratops richardsoni, a dinosaur that lived 76 million years ago, had **15 horns** – more than any other animal.
The **horn moth** lays its eggs in the horns of dead animals. When they hatch, the larvae then feast on the bone...
Flutter this way

When African plated lizards are threatened, they hide in the **grooves** of rocks, then inflate their bodies by filling their **lungs** with air, wedging them so tight nothing can pull them out.

A sloth has special tissues that 'tape' its **lungs** to its rib cage so it can breathe while hanging **upside down**.

Desert tortoises dig **grooves** in the ground to collect rainwater.

The white-lined sphinx moth caterpillar, an animal that lives in the **desert**, sometimes raises its head when it's startled and resembles an Egyptian sphinx.

Velociraptors, turkey-sized **dinosaurs**, could **leap** higher than a football goalpost.

Opossum babies can hang **upside down** from tree branches by their **tails** for short periods of time.

The giraffe has the longest **tail** of any **land animal** – it's as long as a golf club!

The largest **land animal** believed to have ever lived was *Patagotitan mayorum*, a plant-eating **dinosaur** that weighed almost as much as a commercial jet filled with fuel and cargo.

Scientists think the **leaps** and spins that spinner dolphins perform in the air let fellow **dolphins** know where they're going or if danger is ahead.

The United States Navy trains bottlenose **dolphins** and sea lions to find and retrieve equipment lost at sea.

Get to work!

The 'chief mouser' is a cat whose job is to catch rodents for the Prime Minister at 10 Downing Street.

African giant pouched rats are **incredibly intelligent** – they can be trained to sniff out explosives and even some diseases.

At a golf course in Oregon, USA, you can **hire a goat to be your caddie**. The goat will carry golf clubs and balls in a special pack on its back.

Dozens of goats, sheep and donkeys are used to keep the grass trimme

an airport in Chicago, Illinois, USA.
Cows spend about eight hours a day **chewing their cud** – grass that they have already eaten once and regurgitated to eat again.
Munch on this

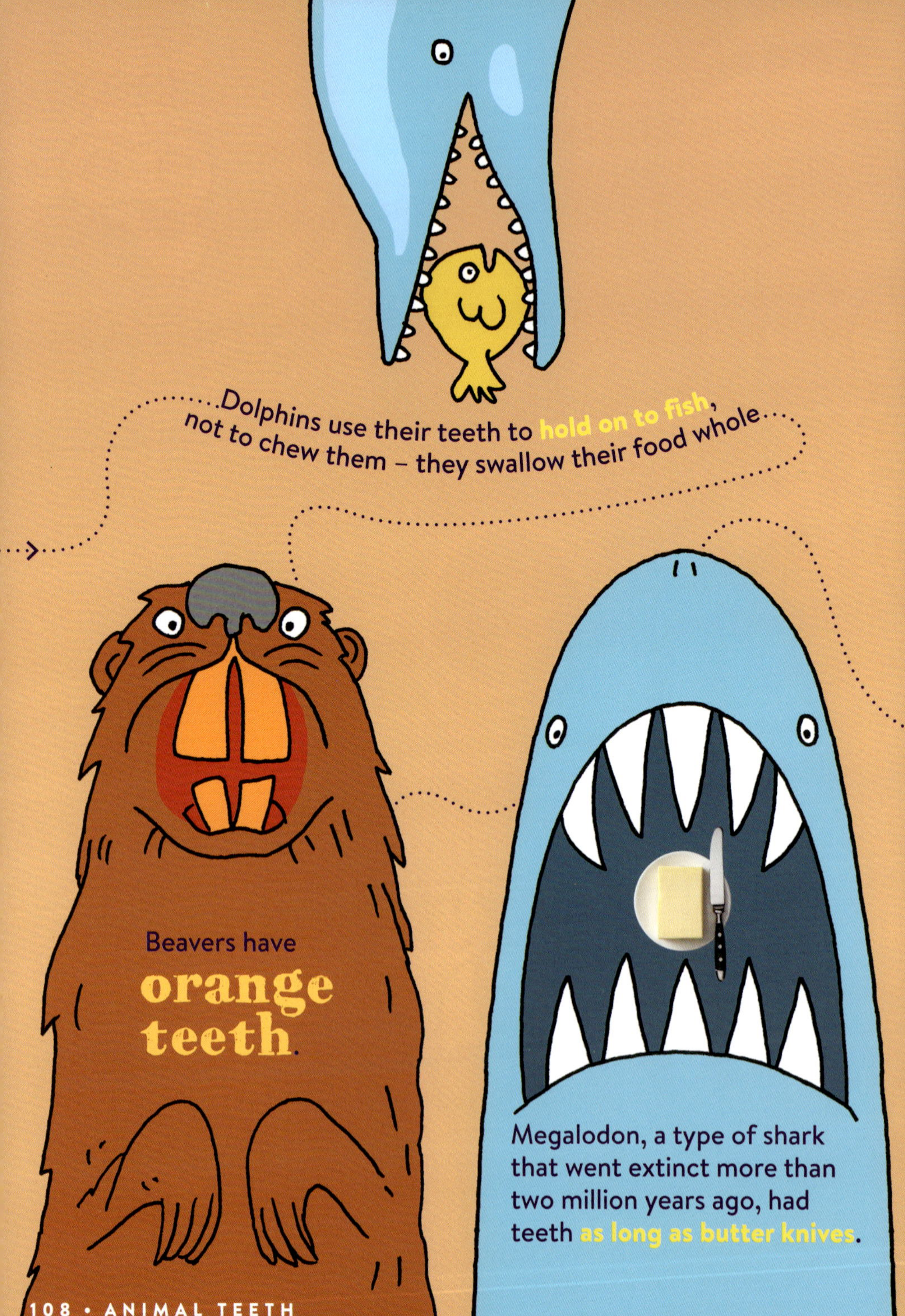

Dolphins use their teeth to hold on to fish, not to chew them – they swallow their food whole.
Beavers have orange teeth.
Megalodon, a type of shark that went extinct more than two million years ago, had teeth as long as butter knives.

Instead of teeth, **microscopic tardigrades** have two daggerlike mouthparts called stylets that they use to pierce their prey and drink their insides.
Look closely
Some monkeys **floss** using bird feathers.
Blast into the past
Go to page 70

An average bed has up to

1.5 million dust mites

living in it...

Straw itch mites, which live in hayfields, **chew on human skin**

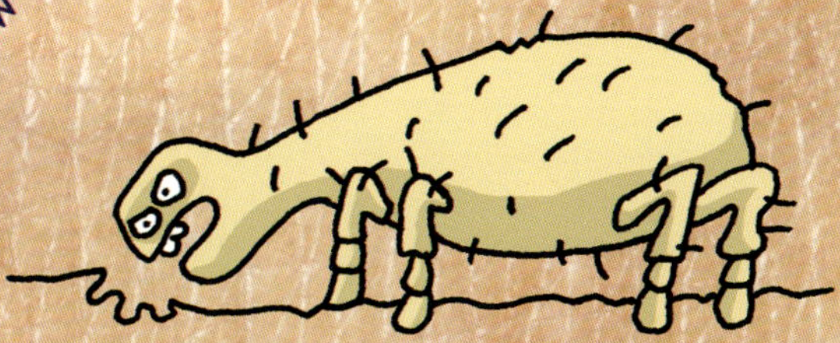

Microscopic male crustaceans called ostracods **vomit glowing mucus** in order to impress potential partners

More on mucus

When whales **clear their blowholes**, they spew out air, water and whale snot.

Go to page 36
Wild about whales
Bonobo mums suck the snot out of their babies' noses
Notable noses

Star-nosed moles can
'smell' underwater
by blowing bubbles and then re-inhaling them, detecting odours of nearby prey.
Sniff, sniff

When stressed, spadefoot toads release a substance that smells like **peanut butter**.

When **honeybees sting**, they send a message to the rest of the hive by producing an odour that smells like bananas.

Create a buzz

Honey badgers, which like to eat honey and bee larvae, have such thick skin they can withstand the venomous stings of African bees.

Venomous black mamba snakes sleep in empty termite mounds.

In their lifetime, a group of 12 honeybees will produce one teaspoon of honey.

A sea lamprey latches on to fish with its suction-cup mouth, then scrapes off their flesh with its sharp teeth so it can feast on their blood.

Cassowaries are large, flightless birds with sharp 10cm-long talons that they use to slice open predators with a powerful kick.

Male kangaroos fight rivals by balancing on their tails so they can kick with both of their feet.

Spiders' feet are covered in millions of tiny hairs designed to help them cling to any surface.

Dolphins are born with just a few hairs around their snouts – these whiskers can look like a moustache.

After biting their victims – which are usually cows and horses – vampire bats use their **tongues** to **lick** up the blood.

Giant anteaters break into **termite mounds** and anthills and use their sticky **tongues** to lick up 35,000 termites and ants in a day.

A **lick** to the eyeball helps a **gecko** keep its eyes clean.

From head to **tail**, the yellow bullhead catfish is covered in over 175,000 tastebuds, 20 times more than humans have in their **mouths**.

Sometimes when a **gecko** loses its **tail**, it will come back to eat it!

When they're getting ready to hibernate, grizzly bears' main priority is eating fatty **foods**. Sometimes, they'll eat the fatty belly and eyeballs of a fish and leave the rest!

Walruses use their **whiskers** to search for **food** on the ocean floor.

Go to page 34

Take a snooze

Sun bears sometimes walk on their hind legs while **carrying their babies** in their arms.

A woman in Virginia, USA, found a black bear **taking a nap in a paddling pool** in her garden.

Pizzly bears are a **rare hybrid** of polar and grizzly bears.

Walk this way
Brown bears **communicate with each other through their feet**! They release a scent from glands on their feet by twisting their paws in the ground in a little dance.
A giant panda can eat up to **38 kilograms of bamboo a day** – that's the same weight as 336 hamburgers!

When camels' **leathery foot pads** hit the ground, they spread out to keep from sinking into the sand.

Geckoes are able to **change the stickiness of their feet** – they can turn it on and off.

The largest known **fossilised dinosaur footprint** ever discovered was about the size of a large bathtub.

Dig up more fossils

A 66-million-year-old fossil was nicknamed '**crazy beast**' by scientists because of its strange features: it had front teeth like a rodent, back legs that splayed out like a crocodile and a hole on top of its snout

Just imagine
Scientists believe fossils of extinct animals like dinosaurs inspired ancient people around the world to believe in **mythical creatures**, such as dragons.

As late as the 16th century, traders brought narwhal tusks from North America and Russia to Europe and claimed they were

UNICORN HORNS

Go to page 100

Giant oarfish can grow to be longer than a pickup truck. They're thought to be the inspiration for tales about **sea serpents**.

In prehistoric Egypt, flamingos that laid eggs on hot salt flats may have been the inspiration for the **phoenix** – a bird that dies by burning up and then is born again from the ashes.

Stories of the **kraken** – a massive sea monster – originated in Scandinavian folklore. The Old Norse words *at kraka* mean to drag downward, which is what tales said the creature did to ships with its giant arms.

The unicorn is the **official national animal** of Scotland.

No horsing around

Until 1976, taxi drivers in London were

equired by law to have food on hand for their horses – even though horse-and-buggy taxis were a thing of the past.

Legendary racehorse **SECRETARIAT** had a heart more than twice as big as the one in an average horse.

And the winner is

...A horse makes enough saliva to fill up **100 fizzy drink cans** every day.

A bulldog named Tillman became famous for being able to

ride a skateboard

by pushing off the ground with his paw, which is how he cruised around parks and even New York City's Times Square.

Woof!

To collect **water** and keep their skin moist, Australian green tree **frogs** create their own fog. They jump from the cool night air to their warm underground burrows, creating moisture.

The neon flying squid can propel itself out of the **ocean** at speeds almost as fast as the world's fastest man, Usain Bolt, can **run**.

When trumpeter swans **run** across the **water** to take flight, it sounds like galloping horses.

When boxer dogs get **excited**, they sometimes 'box' each other with their front paws while balancing on their back legs.

Excited guinea pigs sometimes 'popcorn' – the name for when they **jump** straight up in the air.

Hairy frogfish aren't **frogs** and they don't have hair – they're a fish covered in fleshy spines that walk on the seafloor with their fins!

Something's fishy

The giant bumphead parrotfish uses its oversize forehead to **bump** into rivals near **ocean** coral reefs.

If an alligator is in a Florida manatee's space, the manatee often **swims** up to it and **bumps** it until it moves out of the way.

When a young wallaby senses danger, it often **jumps** into its mother's **pouch** for protection.

The water opossum has a watertight **pouch** that keeps its babies dry while it **swims** in streams and ponds.

One species of batfish looks like it's wearing **bright-red lipstick** on its mouth

Blue tang fish are also known as palette tang because their black markings resemble an artist's palette.
There's a pattern here

A jaguar's spots are called **rosettes** because the jagged circles on its coat resemble roses
Male white-spotted pufferfish impress females by creating patterns on the seafloor and then **decorating them with shells**

Computer scientists created a **barcode-like scanning system** that identifies individual zebras from a photograph

In black and white

Giant pandas sometimes do
HANDSTANDS
when they pee.
Dalmatians have spots not only on their coats, but also inside their mouths.

When **orcas** are born, their bellies and eye patches are pinkish-orange, not white.

A group of penguins on land is called a ***WADDLE***

BALD-FACED HORNETS CAN BUILD NESTS BIGGER THAN BASKETBALLS.

That stings!

Tarantula hawks aren't spiders or birds; they're wasps that have one of the insect world's **most painful stings**.

Scorpions **duel with their venomous tails**; the winner stings and eats its rival...

More venom

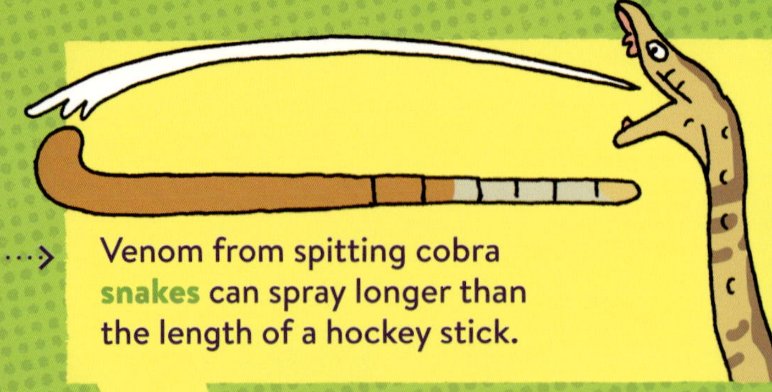

Venom from spitting cobra snakes can spray longer than the length of a hockey stick.

The world's smallest bird egg, laid by the vervain hummingbird, is the size of a pea.

King cobras are the only snakes that build nests for their eggs.

Black herons fold their feathers over their heads to form a makeshift umbrella that creates shade to attract fish in shallow water.

Badgers dig shallow holes outside of their dens to use as toilets.

Galápagos penguins lay their eggs in holes found in lava rocks.

Alligators swallow small rocks to help them stay underwater longer.

Moose dive underwater to eat plants off the bottom of lakes and ponds.

Platypuses search for food at the bottom of ponds and rivers using their supersensitive bills, which can pick up the electric fields produced by their prey.

Ruby-throated hummingbirds flap their wings more than 50 times in one second.

The wings of pterosaurs – flying reptiles that lived at the time of dinosaurs – were not only for flying: they also used them for walking on the ground.

The dinosaur *Spinosaurus* hunted for prey both in the water and on the shoreline like modern-day herons.

A brown pelican can hold three times more food in its bill than in its stomach.

Inside its stomach, a ghost crab has teeth that not only help it digest food, but when ground together, also make a growling noise it uses to scare off predators.

One species of crab, called the coconut crab, uses its serrated front claws like a knife to crack open whole coconuts.

Sidestep this way

Despite their name, hermit crabs are social and can gather and live in groups of more than 100 in the wild

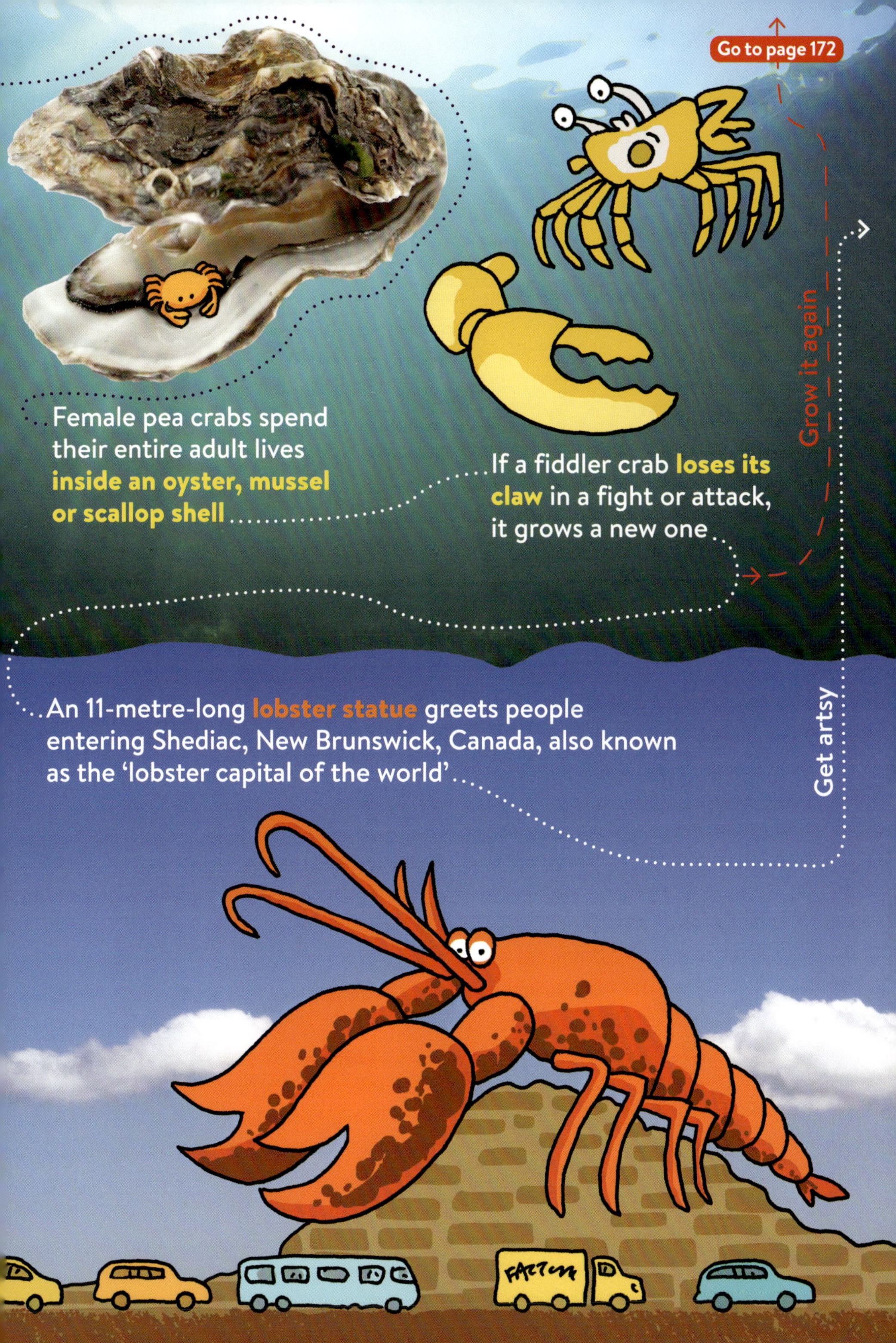

Go to page 172

Female pea crabs spend their entire adult lives **inside an oyster, mussel or scallop shell**

If a fiddler crab **loses its claw** in a fight or attack, it grows a new one

Grow it again

An 11-metre-long **lobster statue** greets people entering Shediac, New Brunswick, Canada, also known as the 'lobster capital of the world'

Get artsy

In 2008, a French artist made **1,600 papier-mâché giant pandas**, one for every panda left in the wild at the time, and displayed them in cities around the world

You can buy **paintings** created by a red panda, rhino or cheetah at a zoo in Houston, Texas, USA.

A statue in Edinburgh honours Wojtek, a **trained brown bear** that helped Polish troops carry supplies during World War II.

Superheroes this way!

An Australian tabby cat named Sally was credited with **saving her owner's life** from a house fire by jumping on him while he was sleeping and meowing loudly, waking him up

Frida, a yellow Labrador retriever, **helped rescue survivors** after an earthquake in Mexico . . .

Soldiers in World War I used glass jars to gather

glowworms

that emitted enough light to read maps and reports at night . . .

On the bright side

Some types of fireflies **flash their lights in sync** to help members of the same group find each other.

The edges of giant clams **glow blue**, helping the algae that live inside them grow.

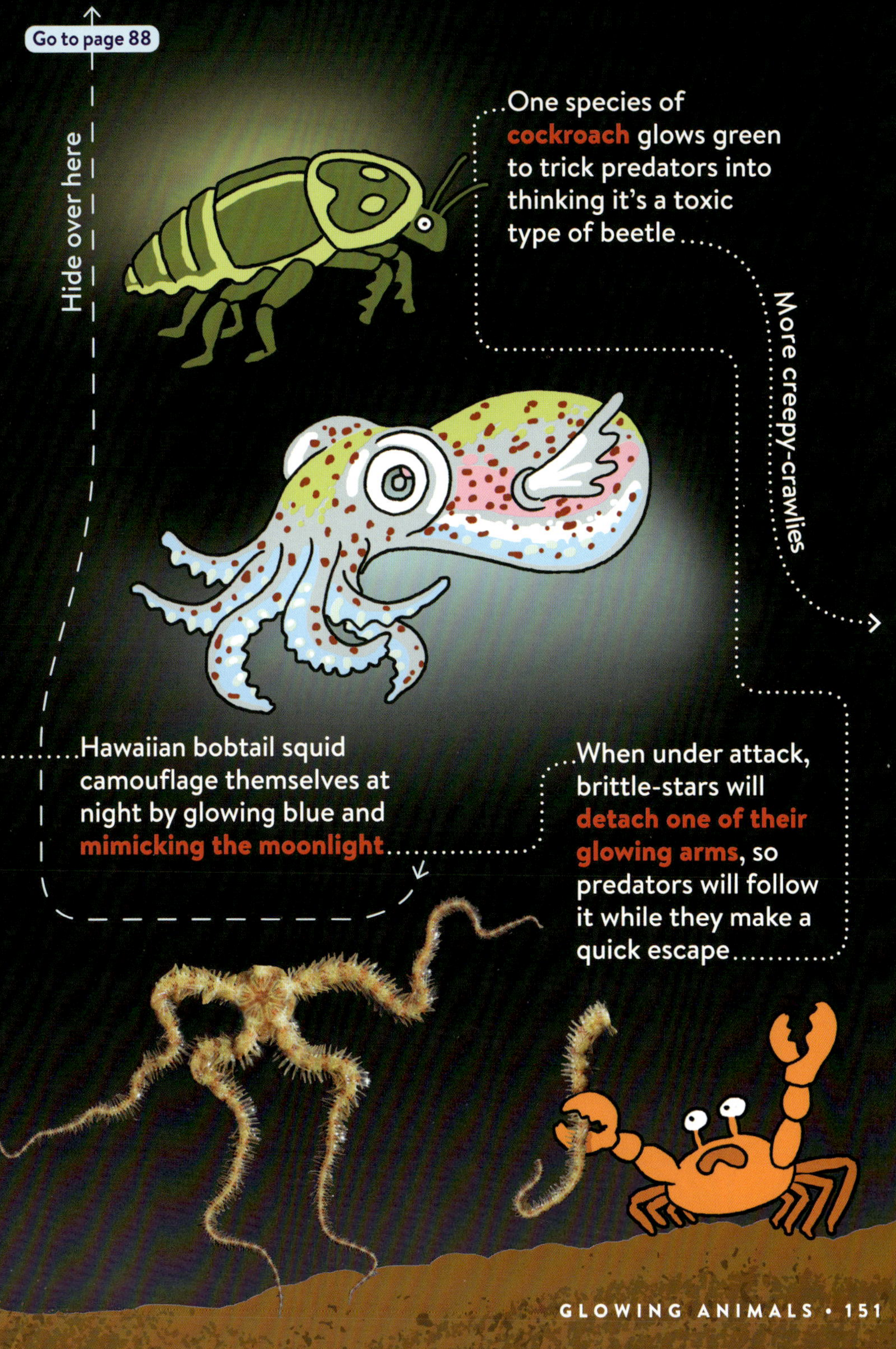
Go to page 88
Hide over here
One species of cockroach glows green to trick predators into thinking it's a toxic type of beetle
More creepy-crawlies
Hawaiian bobtail squid camouflage themselves at night by glowing blue and mimicking the moonlight
When under attack, brittle-stars will detach one of their glowing arms, so predators will follow it while they make a quick escape

The titan beetle can

bite

a pencil in half with its jaws

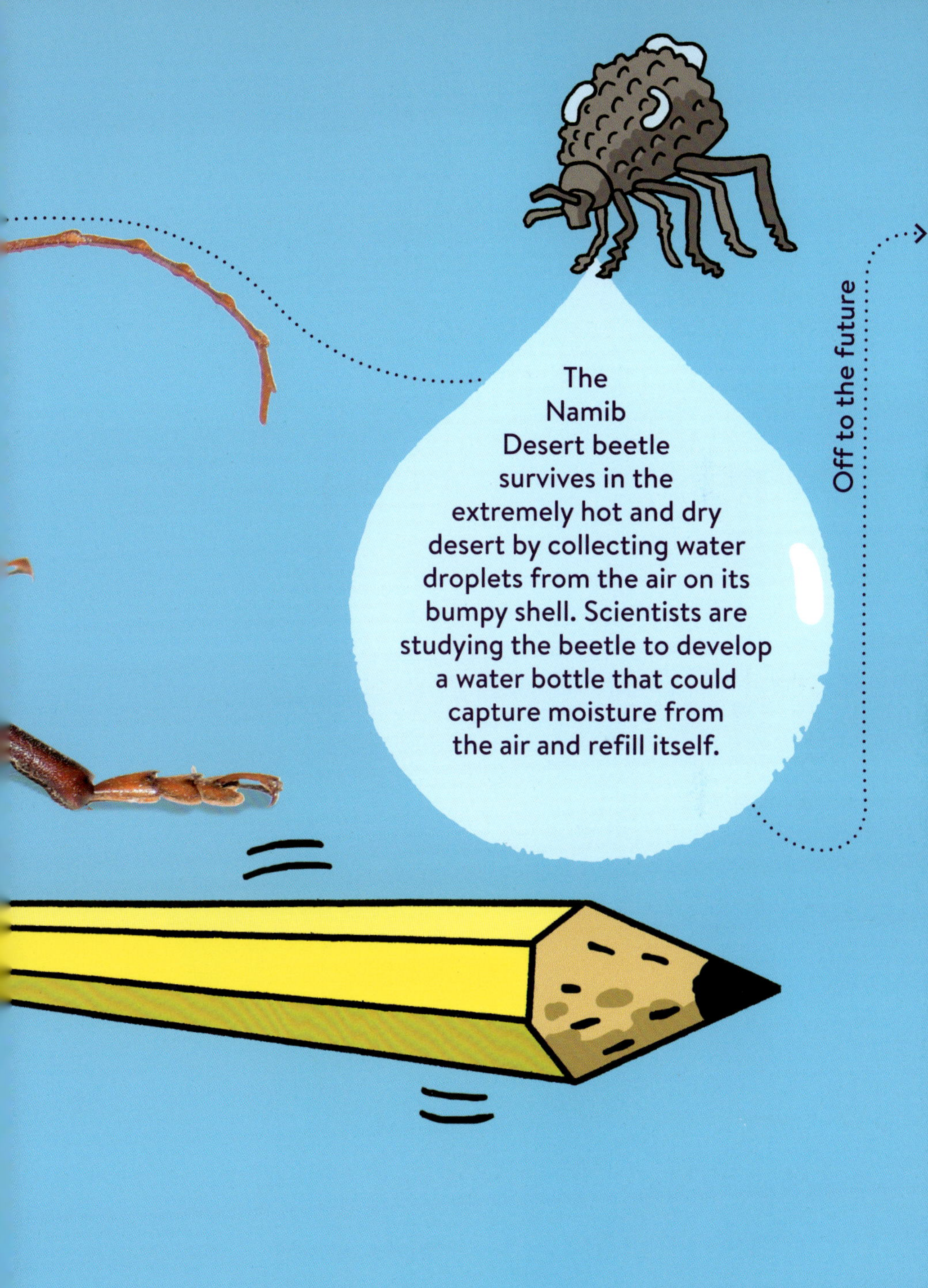

The Namib Desert beetle survives in the extremely hot and dry desert by collecting water droplets from the air on its bumpy shell. Scientists are studying the beetle to develop a water bottle that could capture moisture from the air and refill itself.

Scientists copied the patterns of beaver and sea otter hair to design material for a new warm,
FURRY WET SUIT.
Fabulous fur
Go to page 96
Inspired by an elephant's trunk, scientists invented a flexible roboti

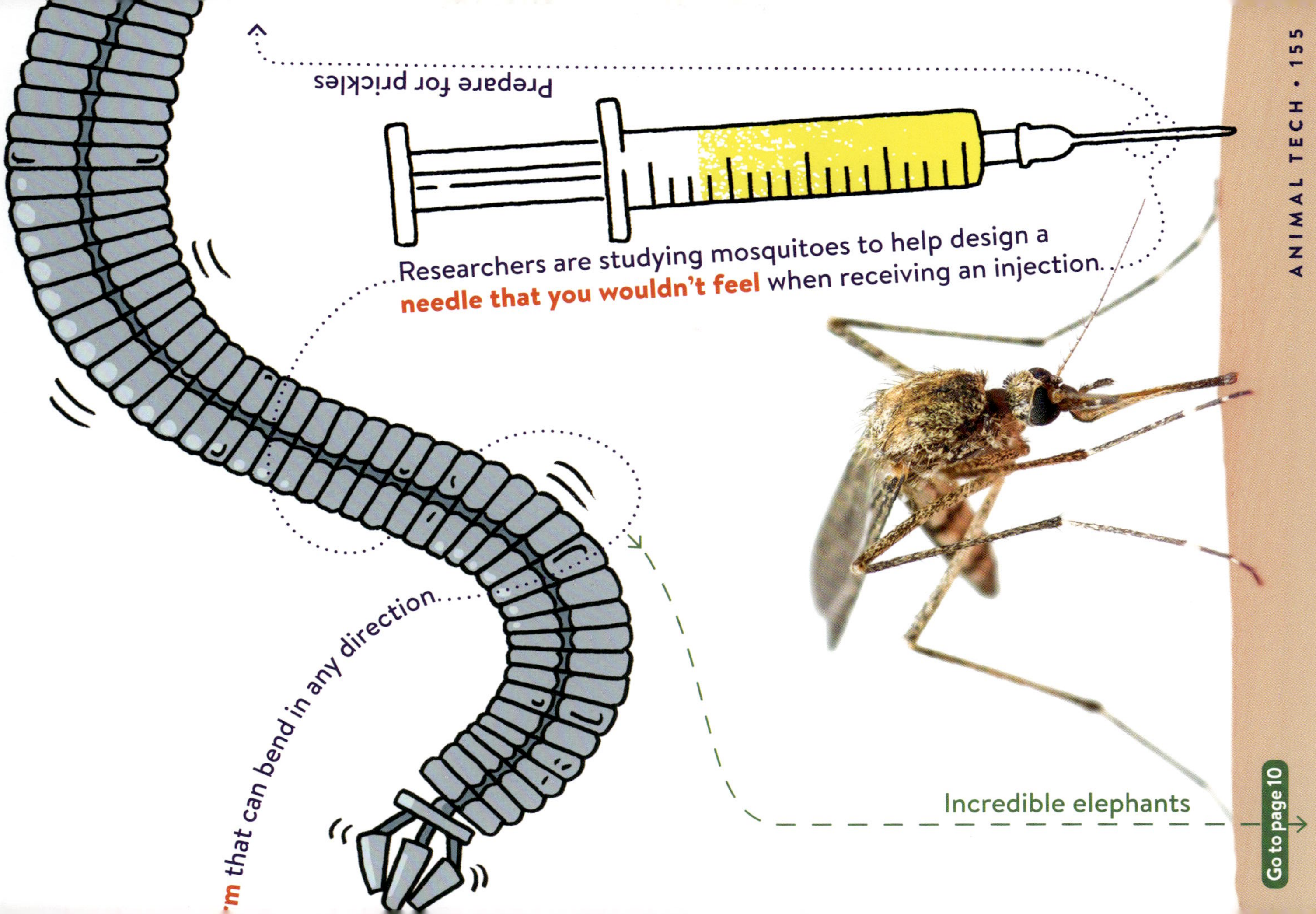

rm that can bend in any direction

Prepare for prickles

Researchers are studying mosquitoes to help design a **needle that you wouldn't feel** when receiving an injection.

Incredible elephants

Go to page 10

Go to page 30

Lots of lizards

Baby hedgehogs are born with **soft spines**. After just a day, the spines become hard and sharp.

Texas horned lizards can inflate themselves with air so the spikes that cover their bodies poke out, making it hard for a predator to eat them.

Porcupines **rattle hollow quills** at the base of their tails to warn predators to back off.

The puss caterpillar's 'hairs' are actually **tiny hollow spines filled with venom**.

The elf owl, **the world's smallest owl**, makes its home inside holes of spiky desert saguaro cactuses.

For something a little softer

Franchesca, an English Angora rabbit, **set a world record** by having fur that was just over 36cm, the longest of any rabbit

In the winter, Arctic foxes sleep with their fluffy tails **wrapped around their bodies for warmth**

An alpaca's **soft wool**, which is shaved to make yarn, is fire-resistant

Go to page 94
Time to clean up
When squirrels fall, they fluff out their BUSHY TAILS for a slower, softer landing.
More rodents
To keep their thick coats clean, South American chinchillas take **baths in fine volcanic dust**.

Capybaras **eat their own poo** in the morning

A rat in New York City earned the nickname

'PIZZA RAT'

after it was filmed carrying a slice of pizza down a flight of subway stairs

Scurry underground

Some animals have unique fingerprints, just like humans – including gorillas, chimpanzees and koalas.

Koalas cool down by hugging trees.

Each wolf pack has a unique howl.

In New York City, two goats wandering along the subway tracks held up commuters for over an hour.

The pygmy shrew has to eat every hour or it will die.

Eastern hognose snakes pretend to die when attacked by a predator, becoming stiff and lifeless, even when poked.

A beaver cuts down an average of 300 **trees** in a year.

Swim down the river

Hyenas **vomit** around their dens and caves... then other members of their **pack** roll in it.

A camel's **spit** is mostly **vomit**, not saliva.

When **attacked**, Sally Lightfoot crabs **spit** water at predators.

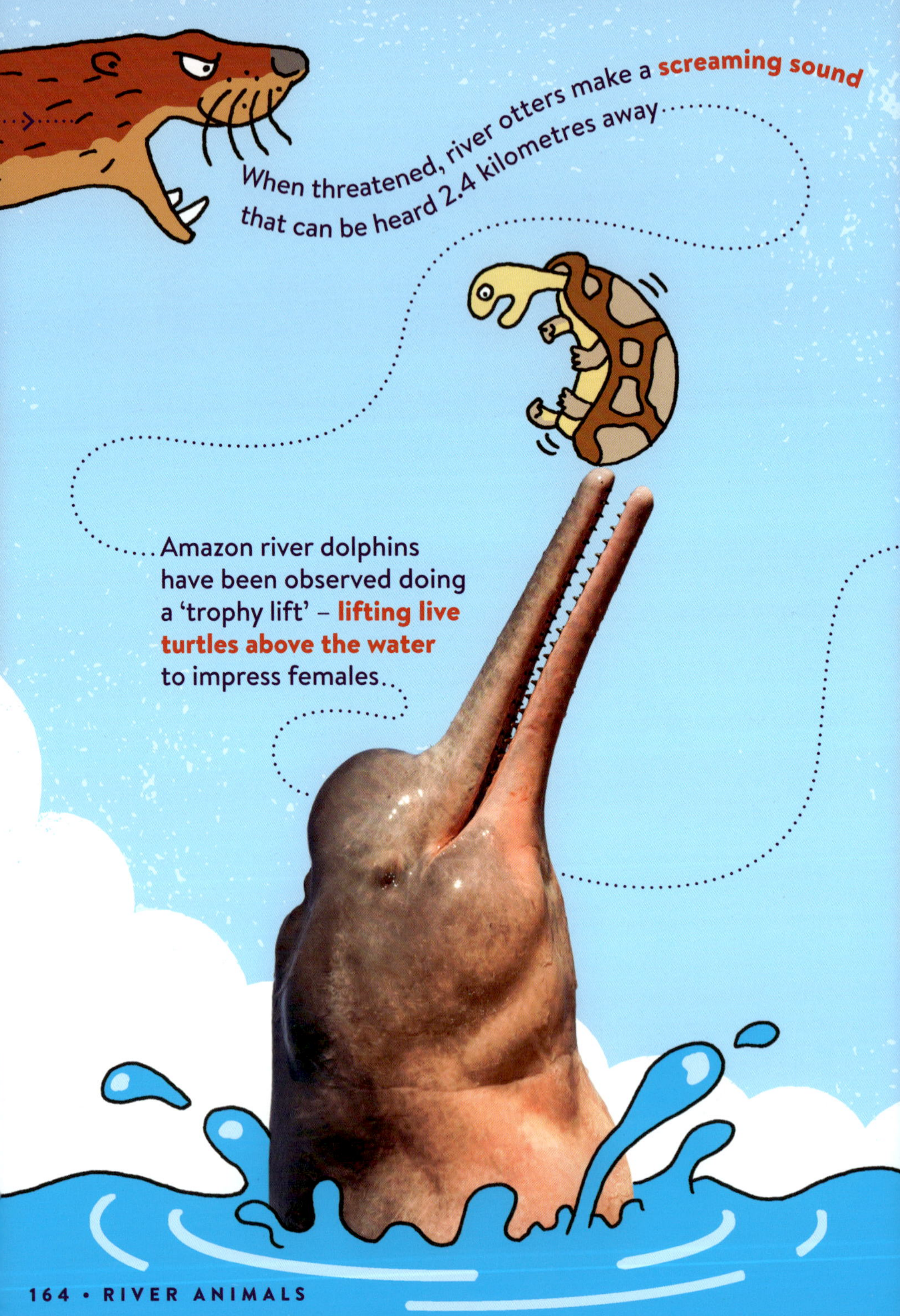
When threatened, river otters make a screaming sound that can be heard 2.4 kilometres away
Amazon river dolphins have been observed doing a 'trophy lift' – lifting live turtles above the water to impress females.

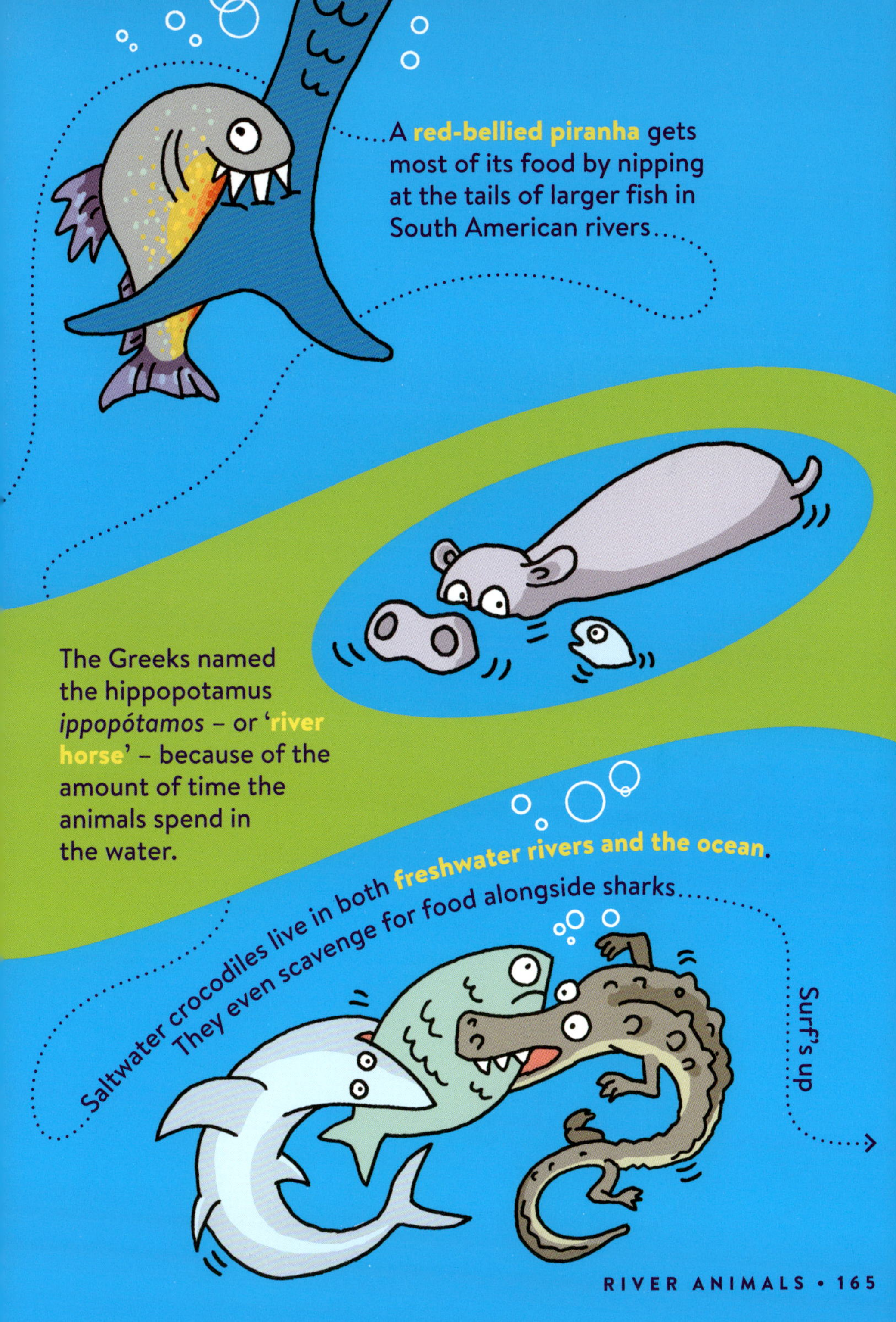

A **red-bellied piranha** gets most of its food by nipping at the tails of larger fish in South American rivers...

The Greeks named the hippopotamus *ippopótamos* – or '**river horse**' – because of the amount of time the animals spend in the water.

Saltwater crocodiles live in both **freshwater rivers and the ocean**. They even scavenge for food alongside sharks...

Surf's up →

Cowries, the shells of molluscs, were **once used as money**

African penguins sometimes dig nests on top of **piles of their own poo** on beaches near Cape Town, South Africa.

Whether a **sea turtle** is a male or female depends on the temperature of the sand where its mother laid her eggs

Turtle-y awesome →

Western painted turtles can **hold their breath** for four months

Need a breather?

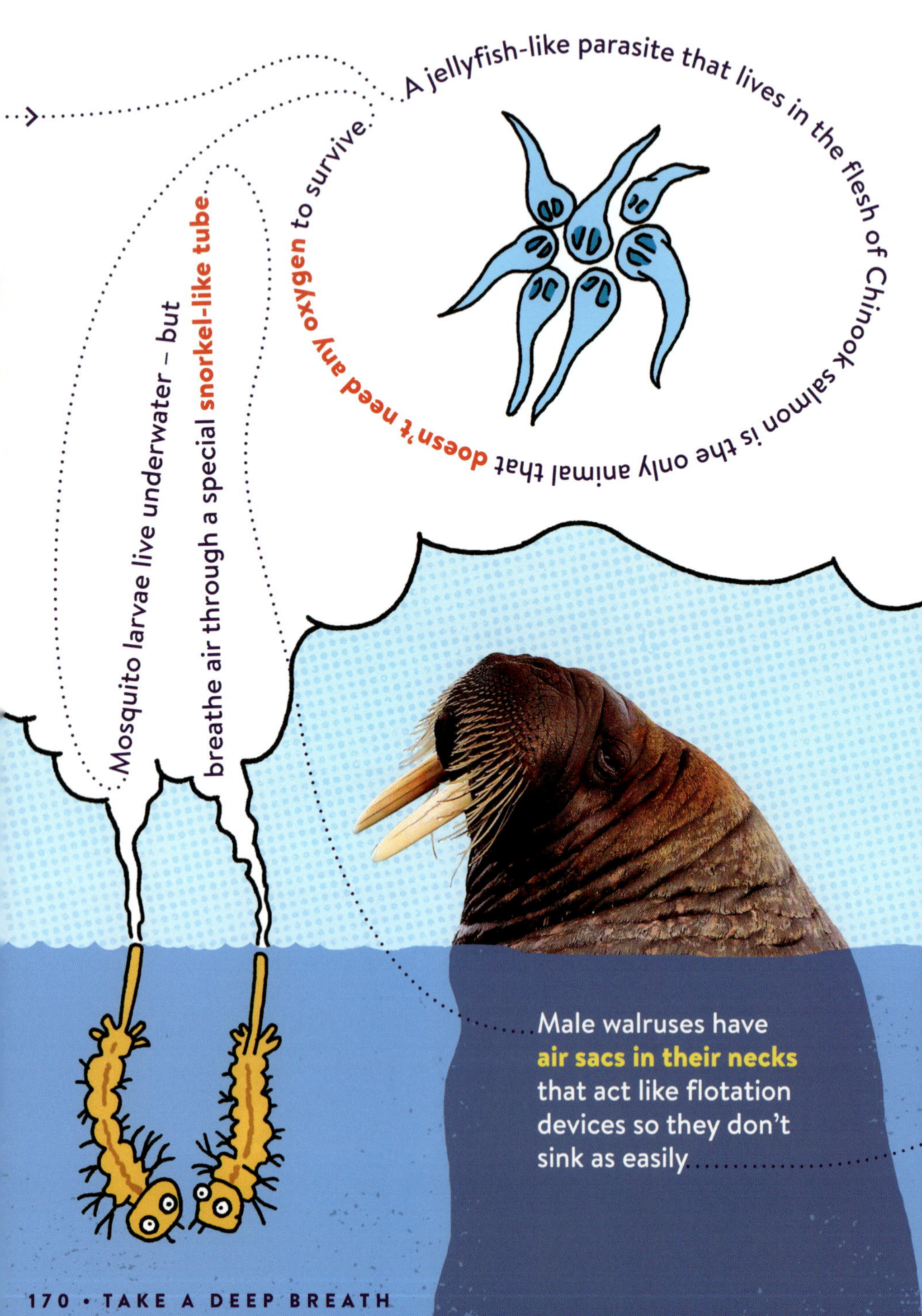
A jellyfish-like parasite that lives in the flesh of Chinook salmon is the only animal that **doesn't need any oxygen** to survive.
Mosquito larvae live underwater – but breathe air through a special **snorkel-like tube**
Male walruses have **air sacs in their necks** that act like flotation devices so they don't sink as easily.

Horses are one of the only mammals that **breathe only through their noses** – not their mouths
Grow on
Axolotls, a type of aquatic salamander, can **regrow their own lungs** after an injury

If their bodies become infected with parasites, some types of sea slugs will chop off their own heads, leave their old bodies behind and **regrow new healthy bodies**

Extraordinary extremities

Some types of **starfish** can grow an entire body from a lost limb.

Cats can spring up to nine times their height from a sitting position.

When standing, the world's tallest dog – a Great Dane named Zeus – stood at the same height as two stacked emperor penguins.

The spine of a cheetah is more flexible than those of other big cats, allowing it to cover the length of a pickup truck with each stride.

Brittle-stars have arms that are flexible and about as long as a tennis racquet.

A seahorse can use its tail to hold onto grasses so it doesn't get swept away in the ocean current.

To help lead her cubs through the savanna's tall grasses, an African lion mother raises her black tufted tail like a flag.

The tails of spider monkey babies act like seat belts. To keep from falling, they wrap their tails around their mothers while swinging through trees.

Capuchin monkeys in Venezuela rub millipedes on their fur because millipedes have special chemicals in them that keep insects away.

Humboldt **penguins** shoot '**poo** bombs' that can fly more than 1.2 metres away.

Every year, a single sea cucumber generates 14 kilograms of **poo**, which it **drops** on coral reefs, keeping them healthy.

Australian pranksters will often jokingly warn tourists about vicious koala bears that may **drop** on them from **above**.

When viewed from **above**, Isabela Island in the Galápagos looks like a **seahorse**.

How smart

Yellow-spotted **millipedes** release a chemical that **smells** like toasted almonds when under attack.

Even though some say the durian fruit **smells** like onion and gym socks, it is one of the **orangutan**'s favourite foods.

Ken Allen, a young **orangutan** at a zoo in California, USA, sometimes unscrewed the bolts of his enclosure, walked around his nursery at night, then locked himself back in before zookeepers noticed.

Honeybees can solve simple addition and subtraction problems.

New Caledonian crows **carve hooks on th**

Go to page 16
Fly this way
nd of sticks to grab grubs better...
Pocket gophers use stones like shovels to build their burrows...
Construction ahead

Some birds use **snakeskin** when building their nests

Arctic foxes grow **colourful 'gardens'** around their dens in the tundra thanks to their poo and urine – which make a rich compost for plants

The ovenbird gets its name from the shape of its nest, which looks like an **outdoor bread oven**

Paper wasps build nests by gathering wood and bits of plants, chewing them, then spitting out the pulp, which dries to form a paperlike product
More gooey stuff
Prairie dogs build special rooms in their burrows that they use as nurseries and even bathrooms!

After licking an object that smells new to them, hedgehogs may produce a **frothy foam** from their saliva and put it all over their bodies, including their spines.

Say what?
their slime trails.
behind in

Tarsiers, a type of primate, communicate with each other through a **high-pitched screech** that predators and humans can't hear.

Koko, a western lowland gorilla, learnt **1,000 words** in American Sign Language

Scientists are using **paw-activated buttons** that sound out words to study whether dogs and cats can 'talk' to humans

Perfect paws

A paw print
of a wild
mammal is
called a
pugmark
Clouded leopards can use their sharp-clawed paws to **han**

side down from branches

Young **HORSESHOE CRABS** swim upside down

The **upside-down jellyfish** – which looks like a plant – rests its main body, or bell, on the seafloor and waves its underbelly up towards the sun to catch food floating by.

The sucker-footed bat is one of the rare bats that don't sleep upside-down – it produces a sweat-like substance so that it can **stick upright** on leaves.
That's a sticky situation

A frog's tongue

isn't sticky – its spit is! When the saliva makes contact with prey – like a fly – it becomes a thin liquid and spreads over the bug, then immediately thickens up, helping the frog keep its grip.

The **waxy monkey frog** makes a waxlike substance that it rubs all over its body to keep from drying out in the sun

The marsupial frog has a **pouch like a kangaroo's** on its back, and it carries its eggs in there until they develop into froglets

The rainforest-dwelling strawberry poison frog is red all over except for its **bright blue legs** – the source of its nickname, the 'blue jeans' frog

When a Budgett's frog is disturbed, it lets out a

shrill scream

Get loud! →

Some frogs lay their eggs on the undersides of leaves that hang over streams and rivers. When they hatch, the tadpoles **plop into the water**.

Explore the rainforest
Go to page 64

Screech owls have a unique way of keeping parasitic insects off their **babies**: they capture wormlike snakes and leave them in the nest to eat the parasites that would otherwise infest the owlets.

Naked mole-rats live in communities ruled by one dominant female; all the other family members take care of her **babies** and even eat her **poo**!

Ants don't have ears – they listen by feeling vibrations with their **legs**.

A giraffe's **legs** and **neck** are the same length.

The giraffe weevil has an extra-long **neck** that it uses like a crane to build a leaf nest for a single **egg**.

During the American Civil War, bat poo was collected from Bracken Cave in Texas, USA, to make gunpowder.

At Bracken Cave in the summer, newborn baby bats cram together to roost in groups of more than 5,000 per square metre.

During the summer, a colony of 3,000 gentoo penguins takes up residence outside 'Penguin Post Office' in Antarctica, the southernmost post office in the world.

Antarctica is the only continent that doesn't have any native ant species.

After female giant water bugs lay their eggs, the males carry the eggs on their backs until they hatch.

More proud papas

Male Darwin's frogs swallow developing tadpoles for two months while they grow, then **cough them out** when they are frogs...
...Ostrich mums and dads take turns sitting on their eggs – males **take the night shift** because their dark feathers make them harder for predators to see...
Seahorse dads are the ones that carry the eggs and give birth to ba
It's getting dark
Go to page 22

Brothers and sisters
ahorses – up to 2,000 at a time!

When walking through their underground tunnels, **naked mole-rats** have to make way for their older siblings
To make sure no one gets lost, shrew siblings **make a chain behind their mothe**
Nine-banded armadillo mothers almost always give birth to **identical quadruplets**

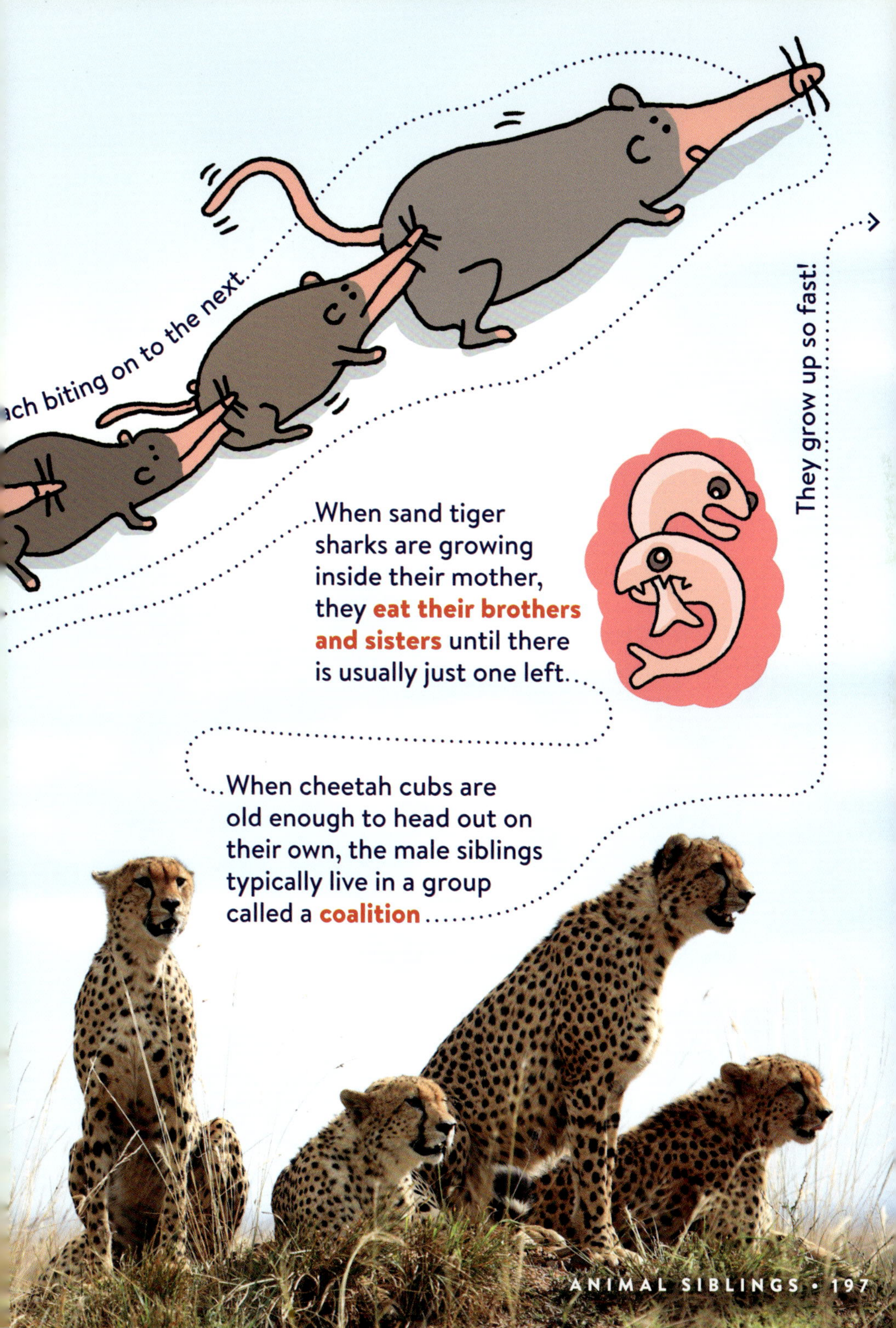

When sand tiger sharks are growing inside their mother, they **eat their brothers and sisters** until there is usually just one left.

When cheetah cubs are old enough to head out on their own, the male siblings typically live in a group called a **coalition**.

The world's longest-living land animal is

Jonathan,

a tortoise that was born before the first petrol car was even invented!

Index

Trademark notices
Frisbee is a trademark of Wham-O

Meet the FACTopians

Julie Beer is an author and editor based in California, USA. Julie has written numerous books for National Geographic Kids on everything from national parks to space to her favourite subject of all – animals! When researching facts for this book, she knew she had to include one about sea otters. Her favourite fact is that sea otters store a special rock under their armpits in case they need to crack open food, such as clams. They're cute and clever!

Andy Smith is an award-winning illustrator. A graduate of the Royal College of Art, London, he creates artwork that has an optimistic, handmade feel. Creating the illustrations for *Animal FACTopia!* brought even more surprises, from lipstick-wearing fish to overheated chameleons! Andy's favourite fact to draw was Tillman the bulldog skateboarding in New York's Times Square. Andy also loved creating the blue tang fish, which looks a lot like his artist palette, but he's also very worried about the titan beetle snapping his pencils in half.

Lawrence Morton is an art director and designer based in London. Though he has worked on some of the world's leading fashion magazines, Lawrence has never had as much fun as when he was working on *Animal FACTopia!* As a left-hander, he was taken by the fact that male cats are more likely to be left-pawed. His favourite fact is that Isabela Island in the Galápagos is shaped like a seahorse!

Sources

Scientists and other experts are discovering new incredible animal facts and updating information all the time. This is why our FACTopia team has checked that every fact in this book is based on multiple trustworthy sources and their work has been verified by a team of fact-checkers. Of the hundreds of sources used in this book, here is a list of key websites we consulted.

News Organisations

askabiologist.asu.edu
bbc.com
cbc.ca
cnn.com
kids.nationalgeographic.com
nationalgeographic.com
nationalgeographic.org
newscientist.com
npr.org
nytimes.com
pbs.org
sciencedaily.com
sciencemag.org
scientificamerican.com
smithsonianmag.com
slate.com
time.com
washingtonpost.com
wired.com

Government, Scientific and Academic Organisations

academic.eb.com
allaboutbirds.org
animaldiversity.org
audubon.org
awf.org
batcon.org
britannica.com
fws.gov
galapagosconservation.org.uk
iucn.org
jstor.org
loc.gov
marinemammalcenter.org
merriam-webster.com
nature.com
ncbi.nlm.nih.gov
nps.gov
oceanconservancy.org
oceanservice.noaa.gov
penguinsinternational.org
pnas.org
royalsocietypublishing.org
sciencedirect.com
spaceplace.nasa.gov

Museums and Zoos

amnh.org
animals.sandiegozoo.org
floridamuseum.ufl.edu
kids.sandiegozoo.org
nationalzoo.si.edu
nhm.ac.uk
seaworld.org
si.edu

Other Websites

akc.org
atlasobscura.com
guinnessworldrecords.com
nwf.org
panthera.org
space.com
worldwildlife.org
wwf.org.uk

Coming Soon!

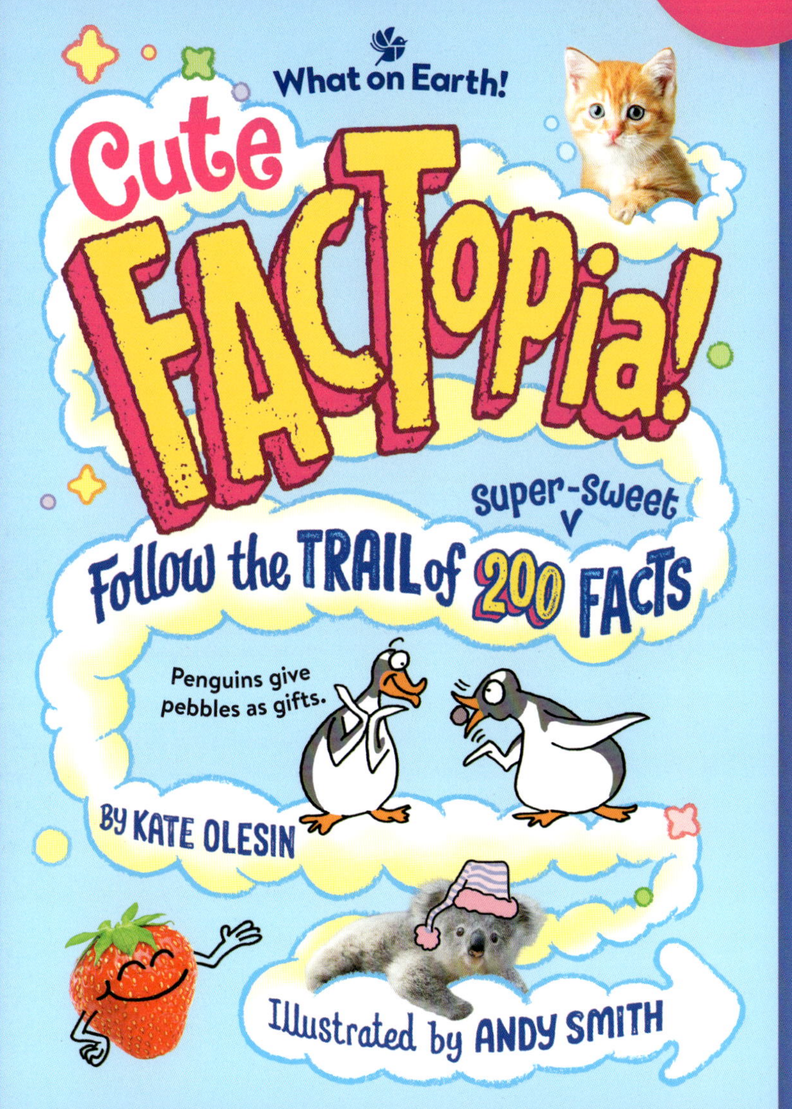

What on Earth!
Cute
FACTopia!
Follow the TRAIL of super-sweet 200 FACTS
Penguins give pebbles as gifts.
BY KATE OLESIN
Illustrated by ANDY SMITH

Picture Credits

The publisher would like to thank the following for permission to reproduce their photographs and illustrations. While every effort has been made to credit images, the publisher apologises for any errors or omissions and will be pleased to make any necessary corrections in future editions of the book.

Cover Images: Penguin Alexey Seafarer/Shutterstock; Chameleon PetlinDmitry/Shutterstock

6 (ctr) Dirk Ercken/Shutterstock; 6 (lo) Lillian Tveit/Dreamstime; 8 Barbara Ash/Alamy; 11 SeDm/Shutterstock; 12 meunierd/Shutterstock; 17 Mike_shots/Shutterstock; 19 Annette Shaff/Shutterstock; 20 Oliver Thompson-Holmes/Alamy; 21 BIOSPHOTO/Alamy; 23 Abhishek Sah Photography/Shutterstock; 24–25 Lillian Tveit/Dreamstime; 27 Horst Bierau/Moment Open/Getty Images; 28–29 Marisa Estivill/Shutterstock; 30–31 Albert Beukhof/Shutterstock; 32–33 Mike Pellinni/Shutterstock; 35 BIOSPHOTO/Alamy; 36 Hany Rizk/EyeEm/Getty Images; 37 Elena Veselova/Dreamstime; 38–39 D. Parer and E. Parer-Cook/Minden Pictures; 41 PetlinDmitry/Shutterstock; 42 takmat71/Shutterstock; 43 Eric Isselee/Shutterstock; 44 Trent Townsend/Shutterstock; 45 Sarah2/Shutterstock; 46 Kuttelvaserova Stuchelova/Shutterstock; 47 Blazej Lyjak/Shutterstock; 50–51 Marko Steffensen/Alamy; 52–53 Sasha Samardzija/Shutterstock; 54–55 Slavianin/Shutterstock; 56–57 Martin Pelanek/Shutterstock; 57 (tail) Valentyna Chukhlyebova/Shutterstock; 58–59 (up) ipolsone/Shutterstock; 59 ctr Petr Ganaj/Shutterstock; 60 Aleksandar Dickov/Dreamstime; 61 Laura Romin/Alamy; 62–63 Pics516/Dreamstime; 64 BIOSPHOTO/Alamy; 67 Kirsten Wahlquist/Shutterstock; 69 Sibmens/Dreamstime; 70 Kerry Hill/Dreamstime; 72 3Dstock/Shutterstock; 73 Luna Vandoorne/Shutterstock; 74–75 Dave Watts/Alamy; 76 iacomino FRiMAGES/Shutterstock; 77 Nikolai Sorokin/Dreamstime; 78–79 (up) Fotoeye75/Dreamstime; 79 (le) effe45/Shutterstock; 79 (rt) Kazakovmaksim/Dreamstime; 80–81 Joe Sohm/Dreamstime; 83 (le) Andrey_Kuzmin/Shutterstock; 83 (rt) Sonsedska Yuliia/Shutterstock; 85 B. Saxton, (NRAO/AUI/NSF) from data provided by M. Goss, et al.; 86–87 (up) IP Galanternik D.U./iStockphoto/Getty Images; 87 Alexey Seafarer/Shutterstock; 88–89 Rich Carey/Shutterstock; 90 Volodymyr Burdiak/Shutterstock; 91 Nerssesyan/Shutterstock; 94 Sergey Uryadnikov/Shutterstock; 95 Jesse Nguyen/Shutterstock; 96 Eric Isselee/Shutterstock; 98 (up) monticello/Shutterstock; 98 (lo) evaurban/Shutterstock; 99 Cubanito/Dreamstime; 100–101 yevgeniy11/Shutterstock; 103 Antonella865/Dreamstime; 105 Dr Neil Overy/Science Photo Library RF/Getty Images; 106–107 Russ Heinl/Shutterstock; 108 Lightfieldstudiosprod/Dreamstime; 109 Somrerk Witthayanant/Shutterstock; 110 Realstock/Shutterstock; 111 (up) Deyangeorgiev/Dreamstime; 111 (lo) Volodymyr Byrdyak/Dreamstime; 112–113 Digital Storm/Shutterstock; 114–115 Astrid Gast/Shutterstock; 116 Erni/Shutterstock; 117 Vidas/Shutterstock; 119 Steve Adams/iStockphoto/Getty Images; 120 (ctr) TangoFoxtrot2018/Shutterstock; 120 (lo) Steven J. Kazlowski/Alamy; 121 Oktay Ortakcioglu/MediaProduction/E+/Getty Images; 123 Eric Isselee/Shutterstock; 125 Ken Backer/Dreamstime; 126 Dotted Yeti/Shutterstock; 128 Aleksandra Stepanova/Dreamstime; 129 Andersastphoto/Dreamstime; 130–131 Austin Paz/iStockphoto/Getty Images; 133 (up) Tamil Selvam/Shutterstock; 133 (lo) Shmelly50/Shutterstock; 134–135 Norbert Probst/imageBROKER RF/Getty Images; 136 (up) Martin Mecnarowski/Shutterstock; 136–137 JovanaMilanko/iStockphoto/Getty Images; 138 blickwinkel/Alamy; 139 Eric Isselee/Shutterstock; 140–141 buddeewiangngorn/123RF; 143 Steve Byland/Shutterstock; 144 back Damsea/Shutterstock; 144 (lo) Kisneborosmaria/Dreamstime; 145 (up le) Muellek Josef/Shutterstock; 145 (up back) Rich Carey/Shutterstock; 145 (lo) incamerastock/Alamy; 146 Artitwpd/Dreamstime; 147 Konrad Zelazowski/Alamy; 148 (door) Aliaksey Dobrolinski/Shutterstock; 148–149 New Africa/Shutterstock; 150 kai egan/Shutterstock; 151 davemhuntphotography/Shutterstock; 152 massdon/Shutterstock; 154 Jason Prince/iStockphoto/Getty Images; 155 nechaevkon/Shutterstock; 156 Brett Hondow/Shutterstock; 157 Larry N Young/iStockphoto/Getty Images; 158 karinabaumgart/123RF; 159 V_E/Shutterstock; 160-161 M_a_y_a/E+_Getty Images; 162 kojoty/123RF; 163 LouieLea/Shutterstock; 164 Coulanges/Shutterstock; 166–167 Iciar Cano Fondevila/Dreamstime; 168–169 scubaluna/iStockphoto/Getty Images; 170 Ondrej Prosicky/Shutterstock; 171 Debra Boast/Dreamstime; 172–173 cbimages/Alamy; 172–173 (back) Lubo Ivanko/Shutterstock; 175 Jacques Descloitres, MODIS LRRT/NASA/GSFC; 176 Daniel Prudek/Shutterstock; 177 Matt Knoth/Shutterstock; 178 (up) Martin Bech/Shutterstock; 178 (lo) Luciana Tancredo/Shutterstock; 180–181 Bruno Pacha/Shutterstock; 182–183 sabine_lj/Shutterstock; 184 Huseyin Faik/Alamy; 186 Laura Dts/Shutterstock; 188–189 Kurit afshen/Shutterstock; 190 Dirk Ercken/Shutterstock; 192 Dennis van de Water/Shutterstock; 195 Azahara Perez/Shutterstock; 197 surbs279/iStockphoto/Getty Images; 198 Morphart Creation/Shutterstock